A Pictorial History of
Brighton

BRIGHTON
BOROUGH COUNCIL

A Pictorial History of
Brighton

DAVID BEEVERS

JOHN ROLES

The Breedon Books
Publishing Company
Derby

First published in Great Britain by
The Breedon Books Publishing Company Limited
44 Friar Gate, Derby, DE1 1DA
1993

ISBN 1 873626 54 1

Printed and bound by Hillman's Printers, Frome, Somerset.
Jacket printed by BDC Printing Services Limited of Derby.

Contents

The terrace of the
Metropole Hotel
photographed by
Bedford Lemere
in 1915.

Acknowledgements

THE majority of photographs in this book are from the collection held by the Royal Pavilion, Art Gallery and Museums, Brighton. The remainder were lent by East Sussex County Libraries, and the authors would like to extend their warmest thanks to John Lake, Elaine Jewell, Hilary Woodard and Stephanie Green for their help and encouragement. The photographs of the Swan Downer School, St Michael's Church, St Martin's Church, St Mary's Church, the Market, the Art School, the Metropole Dining Room, the interior of Grand Avenue Mansions, the Chain Pier Entrance and the Terrace of the Metropole Hotel are reproduced by courtesy of the Royal Commission on the Historical Monuments of England.

Special thanks are due to Maureen Simmonds, who typed the manuscript impeccably, and to Fred Woodley, who cheerfully bore the brunt of making copies of over two hundred photographs.

Introduction

MENTION Brighton to any group of people and they will each have a memory or anecdote about the town. People's perceptions of the town vary greatly. To some it conjures up 'dirty weekends', family seaside holidays, the annual Veteran Car Run, the Royal Pavilion, or the horrors of the Grand Hotel bombing. To others the architectural glories of the Regency squares and terraces, a vision of London by the Sea, Pinky in *Brighton Rock*, or one of the town's many cinematic portrayals. Brighton is all these things and more; it is a place to visit, a place to live, but, above all, it is a place to cherish.

This book aims to provide a glimpse of Brighton as it was, to show how the town has changed, of buildings long gone, of changing fashions and altered lives. It makes no claim to be comprehensive, or even representative, but the images have been selected to illustrate the wealth of Brighton's heritage. Behind the Regency coastal façade the fashionable resort was supported by a multitude of service trades, shops and hotels, theatres and baths, parks and gardens.

The majority of pictures used have not been published before. These evocative images have come from two principal sources: the Brighton collections in Brighton Museum, and the holdings of the Brighton Reference Library. The Museum collections number over 50,000 images, and are growing all the time. They include photographic material from Brighton Borough Council, newspaper archives, records from local photographers, and snapshots donated by the general public. They cover the period from the second half of the nineteenth century right up to the present day. The photographs reproduced here were taken for a variety of reasons. Some were for record purposes, others were to justify demolition, whilst many were taken for simple pleasure. Together they help to form a pictorial record of Britain's premier seaside resort. It is also hoped that these photographs from the past will increase awareness of the importance of what remains. It has justly been said that a town without old buildings is like an old man or woman without a memory. Much of value and interest has been destroyed, partly through ignorance, partly through changing fashions, but above all because of the pressure for new development. What remains to us must be conserved for future generations. As William Morris wrote, we are merely trustees of old buildings. They are not ours to do with them as we like. They belong to those who will come after us. If, in some small way, this book helps to raise an awareness and pride in Brighton as an attractive, vibrant, tolerant and cultured place to live and visit, then it will have been worthwhile.

Popular conceptions of Brighton's history are obscured by the dominance of the Royal Pavilion. It was possible for a nineteenth-century guide book to claim: 'Brighton and its historical associations. Nonsense, there are none!' Much of the literature about the town would have one believe that Brighton's history commences in 1783 with the first visit of the Prince Regent (later George IV) and ends with Queen Victoria's sale of the Pavilion in 1850. Nothing could be further from the truth. In the sixteenth century, Brighton was an important fishing town employing 400 fishermen and 80 boats catching mackerel and herring in the North Sea. By the early seventeenth century it was the largest town in Sussex with a population approaching 4,000 people. In the seventeenth century, French piracy and the growing erosion of the foreshore led the fishing industry to commence a long period of decline which extends into the present century.

With a stagnant economy Brighton's population fell as young men left to make a living elsewhere and the town found itself with growing numbers of dependant and impoverished citizens to support. In 1690, neighbouring parishes provided funds to aid the town. By the middle of the eighteenth century, three-quarters of Brighton's households were too poor to pay rates. Contemporary descriptions record 'the ruins of a large fishing town' with 'here and there houses left deserted and walls tumbling down'. Brighton's fishing industry did not die out completely but became increasingly marginal to the town's economy. By the latter half of the eighteenth century it was increasingly regarded as a quaint tourist attraction.

Rescue was at hand, however. By the 1740s, visitors began to visit Brighton in the search for a health cure. The emergence of a moneyed middle class growing out of the first stirring of early industralisation was the stimulus to this. Inland spas such as Bath, were already an established part of the routine for wealthy landowners and growing numbers of the professional and commercial classes. The first evidence of people coming to Brighton for a health cure comes in 1641 when Mary Askall is described in the parish burial register as 'a woman who came for the cure'. The first reference to sea bathing at Brighton occurs in a letter written by a Sussex clergyman in 1736 and there are bathing machines in use by 1754. Dr Richard Russell was a doctor from Lewes and a great self-publicist who extolled the virtues of both the sea-water cure and of Brighton in particular. In 1776 the *Gentleman's Magazine* remarked: 'Brighton is a small, ill-built town, situated on the sea coast, at present greatly resorted to in the summer season by persons labouring under various diseases, for the benefit of sea bathing and drinking sea water; and by the gay and polite on account of the company which frequent it at this season . . .' Visitors needed lodgings, they expected facilities like theatres, libraries and assembly rooms, all of which provided investment opportunities. Because of its proximity to London, Brighton was accessible to visitors, and its depressed economy meant both land and labour were cheap, offering opportunities for Lewes-based speculators and developers to invest in the town. Samuel Shergold, also from Lewes, built assembly rooms in 1754, two circulating libraries were in existence by 1760, the first baths opened in 1769, and a purpose-built theatre in 1774.

Initially, visitors occupied cramped and dingy rooms in existing houses in the Old Town. A few larger houses were built for more important visitors, Marlborough House being one of the first, in 1765. By the 1780s pressure on land was growing and buildings began to spill out of the Old Town on to the surrounding fields. Initially terraces appeared to the north and east of the Steine which was fast becoming a fashionable promenade.

Brighton was already Britain's largest seaside resort when the Prince of Wales (later George IV) first visited the town in 1783. The building of the Marine Pavilion from 1786 gave the royal seal of approval to an already successful town.

By the 1820s the town had experienced 20 years or more of very rapid growth with the population rising nearly eight-fold to 25,000. But facilities were not keeping pace with the growing number of people. Big estates were commenced at either end of the town and although neither Brunswick Town nor Kemp Town were financially successful, these architect-designed self-contained 'towns' containing their own shops, stabling and churches represent the most grandiose examples of town planning in the early nineteenth century. The large houses of Lewes Crescent or Brunswick Square suited the new fashion for entertaining at home on a lavish scale. These became the fashionable areas and the earlier developments in the centre of the town lost popularity and became boarding and lodging houses. At the same time purpose-built hotels (as opposed to public houses which offered rooms) began to appear. The Royal York Hotel opened in 1819, followed by the Royal Albion in 1826, and the Bedford in 1829.

Brighton's rapid growth had slowed by 1841 but the opening of the railway line from London provided a further stimulus. The train was cheaper, quicker and more comfortable than horse-drawn coaches but, more significantly, the train could carry vastly more passengers. The first excursion trains ran during Easter 1844. In one week in 1850, 73,000 passengers were brought to Brighton and, on Easter Monday 1862, over 132,000 people took the train to Brighton. This new influx of visitors provided a particular range of employment opportunities for the townspeople. There was a large demand for building workers, transport and retailing staff, and for domestic servants. The growing population led to the encroachment of the town up the surrounding hillsides with rows of medium-sized terraced houses and larger detached villas.

Brighton developed an unusual demographic structure with signficantly more women than men since the town provided opportunities for respectable single women of all levels of society to earn a living, something that was rare in the nineteenth century. Working-class women, for instance, could be employed as laundresses, whilst middle-class widows and spinsters could earn a living running boarding and lodging houses, or private schools.

As the nineteenth century wore on the holiday habit spread down the social scale due to economic, social and legislative changes. Growing numbers of day-trippers came to Brighton. These visitors were very different from the fashionable clientele Brighton was used to. They had little money to spend (it had gone on their travel) and they wanted to be entertained cheaply. In 1857 a contemporary referred to 'the miserable sight (on summer Sundays) of poor London artisans and their families who have been beguiled by the promise of 'eight hours at the seaside', to come down for 3s 6d each, to Brighton of all places in the world'. To these visitors the beach became the centre of activity with musicians, Punch and Judy shows, acrobats, tin type photographers, and other entertainments. In the words of a contemporary rhyme:

'I took the train to Brighton — I walked beside the sea,
And thirty thousand Londoners were there along with me,
We crowded every lodging, and we lumbered each hotel,
Sniffed the briny for an appetite and dined extremely well'.

There were those who argued that these trippers brought little economic benefit. The *Brighton Gazette* argued that 'it is to yield to false sentiment to sacrifice the interests of the town to the rabble who are here today and gone tomorrow and leave nothing behind them but the injured feelings of friends and patrons'.

New speculative attractions began to appear. In 1823, the Chain Pier was opened as a landing stage but it soon became a fashionable promenade. The West Pier, designed by Eugenius Birch and opened in 1866, was followed by the Aquarium in 1872, Volk's Electric Railway in 1883, including the fanciful 'Daddy-Long-Legs' extension in 1896, the Palace Pier in 1899, and a string of theatres and music halls.

Behind the seafront lay another Brighton, a town of high density, low-quality housing and of industrial foundries and workshops in the North Laine. Attempts to provide proper services and better housing were begun after Incorporation in 1854.

The spiritual needs of the townspeople were also considered. The increase in population in the nineteenth century led to an unprecedented growth in church building. In the 1820s the Anglican establishment was seen to be in danger as the buildings of the Church of England were outnumbered by those of other denominations. The situation was partially remedied by the building of proprietary chapels (that is chapels built as private speculations by which pews or 'sittings' were allocated according to the number of shares in the chapel bought by each shareholder or proprietor), but these effectively excluded the poor. The vicar of Brighton, Henry Wagner, was concerned to provide church accommodation for those excluded from the proprietary chapels or the parish church. He initiated, or partially financed, the building of six new churches, all of which had free pews set aside for the poor. His son, Arthur, the famous Father Wagner, the High Church sacramentalist, built, largely at his own expense, a further five new churches, of which two, St Bartholomew's and St Martin's, are architecturally of national importance.

Much of the basis of political life in nineteenth-century Brighton lay between those favouring the development of resort facilities to attract visitors and those who wished to retain middle-class residential exclusivity. The difference, perhaps, between brash Brighton and staid Hove. The author of *Brighton in the Golden Reign* (1897) remarked that 'Life in Hove is tranquil and ornate . . .The sound of a concertina in Hove would paralyse the local police with horror. Even the harmless necessary piano-organ is tabooed, so exceedingly fastidious and refined are the people'.

Brighton's growth continued into the twentieth century with the combined population of Brighton and Hove reaching 160,000 by 1901. The town was, however, not in good shape and there was perceived to be a general aura of stagnation and decay. New projects such as the Palace Pier remained unfinished and despite a final flurry of royal patronage with Edward VII's visits to the Sassoon family, it was increasingly felt that the town needed a new direction.

In 1928, Brighton extended its boundaries to take in much surrounding downland. Suburban Brighton continued to grow with the added stimulus of the electrification of the railway to London in 1932-33. New private and council housing estates were built, the Aquarium was remodelled and a series of road widening schemes were to alter dramatically the appearance of many of the town's major shopping streets. The guiding light behind much of this was Alderman Sir Herbert Carden. Inspired by the recently erected Embassy Court, Carden advocated the demolition of the entire seafront from Hove to Kemp Town and its replacement with what he took to be more appropriate modern architecture. Even the Royal Pavilion 'that complete anachronism in a modern age' was under threat. Carden's proposals were fortunately resisted. The *Sphere* (July 1935) stated: 'Sir Herbert, thinking in terms of white concrete and flagpoles seems to forget there is a Regency Brighton as well, and that a large proportion of the visitors to Brighton go there because of these things.'

The outbreak of World War Two prevented comprehensive redevelopment, but in 1945 Hove Council was still proposing to demolish Brunswick Square and Terrace, actions which it was claimed 'would in no way alter the character of the town'. This led to the creation of the Regency Society of Brighton and Hove and a number of other amenity groups to defend the towns' historic heritage.

As we move towards the end of another century, Brighton faces new challenges. Much has changed, the West Pier has become derelict, the Palace Pier no longer has a theatre, churches and many cinemas have vanished. Significant losses include the Regent Cinema, the Central National Schools, and Attree Villa in Queen's Park. The Churchill Square shopping development, the Conference Centre, the Kingswest Boulevard, and the Marina have changed the public face of the town, although not necessarily for the better. Piecemeal redevelopment continues to erode the town's stock of historic buildings.

On a more optimistic note, the successful restoration of the Royal Pavilion, and an official recognition of the need to conserve the town's architectural heritage as recognised in the latest Brighton Borough Plan, bode well for the future. Not everyone would agree with William Cobbett, writing in 1832, who described Brighton as 'certainly surpassing in beauty all other towns in the world', but many who come to live in Brighton, or visit it, grow to love and cherish its history; its buildings and its people.

The ʃ

This view of the entrance to the Chain Pier, *c.*1890, shows that the pier was only 13ft across. The suspension chains can clearly be seen. The two toll kiosks were erected in 1872 to replace the original toll house at the entrance to the Chain Pier Esplanade which were destroyed by the building of the Aquarium. The Chain Pier's narrow walkway and lack of facilities meant it lost popularity to the newer attractions like the West Pier (1866) and Aquarium (1872). Attempts to revive it included a plan by the pier engineer,

front

Eugenius Birch, for the addition of a gigantic Marine Kursaal or winter garden at the head of the pier, but this scheme foundered following Birch's death and through lack of finance. Following the pier's destruction, the two toll houses were removed to the new Palace Pier. The site of the Chain Pier is marked by a plaque on the sea wall above the Aquarium Terrace.

The Chain Pier in the 1880s. Designed by Captain Samuel Brown primarily as a landing stage, the pier opened in 1823 and rapidly became a great favourite with local people and visitors alike. The pier became a popular promenade with small kiosks in the pylons selling souvenirs and offering silhouettes. The pier was closed to the public on 9 October 1896 when it was declared unsafe. Less than two months later it was gone, destroyed in a fierce storm.

The entrance to the Chain Pier in the late 1860s. There were separate entrances for subscribers and non-subscribers; the toll-house itself is just visible on the far right. Once through the gates, visitors could promenade along a quarter of a mile-long esplanade under the cliff to the pier itself. The stall to the left of the entrance is offering tea and cakes to passers-by. The entrance was swept away when Madeira Drive and the Aquarium were constructed in 1871. The Chain Pier was the first seaside pier to be built. It was originally intended as a landing stage for boats, but soon became used as a fashionable promenade.

The view looking towards the shore from the head of the Chain Pier. From an early date the pylons were occupied as small kiosks selling souvenirs and tickets. Small slot machines are visible in this view which dates from the 1880s.

The collapse of the Chain Pier during the storm of 4 December 1896 occurred at about 10.30 pm. The following day, newspaper accounts helped to convey the drama: 'Suddenly, amidst the roaring of the waves and the howling of the wind, the pier shivered convulsively from end to end; and in a few moments the entire structure had collapsed . . .The sea was strewn with the great mass of wreckage, the hugh weather-worn baulks of timber being seen, in the driving rain and salt spray, riding like phantom boats upon the white crests of the waves.'

The West Pier was built between 1863-66 to the designs of Eugenius Birch, the most celebrated of all pier architects. The contractors were R.Laidlaw and Sons of Glasgow. As originally built, the pier was 1,115ft long and was embellished with two toll houses at the landward end, twin kiosks for shelter in the centre, and ladies' and gentlemen's retiring rooms at the pier head. These were decorated with minarets and other Oriental motifs derived from the Royal Pavilion, a daring choice in the 1860s when such motifs were highly unfashionable. Ornamental weather screens were provided at the seaward end, whilst underneath the pier head were landing places for steamers and boats. The pier was lit at night by gas standards. In 1866, the *Brighton Examiner* reported: 'We look upon the structure as artistic and elegant, outrivalling everything of the kind in this country, and perhaps the world.' This photograph, of about 1880, shows the pier before its later embellishments.

The West Pier at the height of its popularity in the late 1920s. The central windshield was added in 1890. In 1893 the pier head was widened, a landing stage added and a new pavilion built at the seaward end; this became a theatre in 1903.

View of the West Pier looking towards Regency Square in about 1930. The concert hall in the centre was added in 1916. It is interesting to observe that Oriental motifs have been abandoned and the building is in a rather heavy-handed *beaux arts* classical style, with just a touch of fantasy on the roof. The concert hall suffered from water penetration during high seas and the orchestra pit was frequently flooded. In addition, it was not unknown for singers' dresses to be blown around their necks when strong winds gusted through the microphone holes in the stage. Note the absence of deck chairs and the free seating along the outer railings. These seats were retained until after World War Two.

The West Pier dodgem track in 1939. During World War Two, the pier
was cut in two to prevent its use for an enemy landing. It
was restored after the war and the theatre was converted into an amusement
arcade. The dodgems were a popular feature at the landward
end of the pier.

The clock tower and gateway to the Aquarium were added in
1874 to the designs of Eugenius Birch; the ironwork was made
in Glasgow by Laidlaw and Sons. At the four corners of the
entrance were bronze statues of the seasons designed and
manufactured in Paris by Messrs Barbezat. Both tower and
entrance were demolished in 1928 when the Aquarium was
remodelled by the Borough Engineer, David Edwards. The new
Aquarium opened in 1929.

The Aquarium was designed by the pier engineer Eugenius Birch and built between 1869-72 at a cost of £130,000. The Gothic aquarium hall, illustrated here, still survives. It is 224ft long with back-lit tanks, one of which was big enough to house the largest whale. The interior, with Bath stone columns, has carved capitals of marine life designed by H.R.Pinker of London. The architect and historian Goodhart-Rendel commented: 'I have never heard justice done to the adroit detail of those strange Victorian galleries from which Victorian children . . .gazed with awe upon the wonders of the deep.'

A 19th-century photograph of the table-tanks off the main Aquarium corridor. The main tanks can be seen in the distance.

The conservatory at the Aquarium was completed in 1872. It consisted of a glazed top-lit gallery 160ft long, the sides of which were covered with an artificial stone known, after its inventor, as Pulham rockwork. This consisted of crushed brick and cement which could be moulded for form boulders. James Pulham was commissioned to supply the artificial rocks, formed as a fernery, waterfall, and 'fairy cave' in 1872. At the extreme end of the conservatory a stream of water was intended to illustrate the breeding of salmon and freshwater fish.

The entrance court of the Aquarium was built in what was called a Pompeian style between 1869-72. The frieze inscription reads: 'And God said, Let the water bring forth abundantly the moving creatures that hath life.' This photograph was taken just prior to demolition.

The demolition of the Aquarium entrance in 1928.

The demolition of the entrance court of the Aquarium in 1927. The photograph bears a passing resemblance to an excavated Roman bath.

Two demolition contractors posing in the Aquarium clock tower in 1928.

Between 1927-29 the Aquarium was remodelled and partly rebuilt to the designs of David Edwards, the Borough Engineer. Twin kiosks in a neo-classical style replaced the distinctive clock tower and a new entrance hall, restaurant and concert hall were provided. The redesigned terrace housed a bandstand and ballroom. This photograph, taken on 12 June 1929, shows a crowd awaiting the arrival of the Duke of York for the official opening.

The opening of Volk's Railway at midday on 4 August 1883. The brainchild of the inventor, Magnus Volk, this was the first public electric railway in Great Britain. The small cars containing up to ten passengers progressed along a narrow track built on the beach and extending for about 300 yards from opposite the Aquarium. The power for the railway was provided by a small generator allowing the car to reach a maximum speed of six miles per hour. The opening ceremony saw the Mayor (Alderman A.H.Cox on the right) and a variety of other dignitaries driven by Magnus Volk himself (on the left in a peaked cap).

The extraordinary Brighton and Rottingdean Seashore Electric Railway was devised by Magnus Volk. Its car on stilts, nicknamed the 'Daddy Long Legs' for obvious reasons, was designed to run on track across the beach from Paston Place to Rottingdean. Current was conveyed to the motors on the deck by an overhead wire. The inaugural ceremony took place on a sunny Saturday, 28 November 1896. The car, christened 'Pioneer', contained the Mayor, Alderman John Blaker, the Mayoress and most of the Town Council, Brighton's two MPs, representatives from Hove and Rottingdean, and the co-engineer of the scheme, Mr St George Moore, the architect of the Palace Pier. The trip to Rottingdean, a short wait and the return journey, took less than an hour and was followed by lunch and speeches in the newly completed Madeira Road Shelter Hall.

Another view of the Brighton to Rottingdean Seashore Electric Railway. The line's route meant the cars were raised above the rails on stilts. Each leg was 23ft long and power was drawn from an overhead wire.

The strange looking railway made its inaugural run on 28 November 1896. When the tide was in, the progress of the car was slowed considerably. Within a week of its opening, the storm which destroyed the Chain Pier wrecked the landing stages and overturned the car itself. Following repairs the line continued in operation until 1901 when the Corporation built concrete groynes to prevent cliff erosion and there was no means of carrying the line over these groynes. In 1901, in compensation, Volk was allowed to extend his original beach railway to Black Rock.

Part of Volk's Railway ran on a wooden viaduct above the beach, providing an enthralling ride in rough weather. Subsequent movement of the pebbles has raised the beach profile and the effect of an overhead railway has been lost. This photograph shows the section east of the Banjo Groyne in 1935.

The Rottingdean Pier of the Seashore Electric Railway with 'Pioneer' preparing to depart. The generating room can be seen under the pier. Even after the demise of the railway in 1901, the pier remained until 1910, as a sad reminder of what had once been.

The original Aquarium station for Volk's Railway in 1912. The station is busy and a queue is visible through the glass screen waiting to pay their 4d return fare for the trip to Black Rock. Many were no doubt attracted by the daily flights in a sea-plane offered by the pioneer aviator, Claude Grahame-White, from a hanger at Paston Place. The flights took place in the last week of July 1912 and were sponsored by the *Daily Mail* newspaper as part of a 'Wake up England!' tour. The old station was reconstructed as part of the revamping of the Aquarium in 1929-30, but it, too, was demolished in 1940. A redundant tram shelter was brought into operation after the end of the war to act as a new Aquarium terminus.

The Palace Pier was built for the Brighton Marine Palace and Pier Company by the engineer R.St George Moore between 1891-99. In 1901 the landing stage and pier head pavilion were added. The pavilion contained a theatre and concert hall, together with a dining room, smoking room, and reading room, which were added in stages between 1901-06. The pier's ornamental ironwork and the onion domes on the pier head pavilion were inspired by Oriental motifs from Nash's Royal Pavilion. In 1901, the *Brighton Herald* described the pier head pavilion as 'a veritable eastern palace'. It continued: 'The scheme of colour is truly Oriental and the brilliant electric light arrangement show it up in all its gorgeousness and splendour.' As originally constructed, the clear deck was intended for promenading. The photograph was taken in 1901.

The ceremony marking the driving of the first screw-pile of the new Palace Pier in November 1891. The Brighton Marine Palace and Pier Company was formed in 1889 in order to erect a new pier opposite the Old Steine to replace the ageing Chain Pier which the new company acquired in 1891 with the aim of demolition. The great storm of 1896 made this unnecessary but left the company with financial difficulties as the Chain Pier wreckage damaged the West Pier and Volk's Railway, causing expensive compensation claims. Consequently, the pier did not open to the public until May 1899.

A photograph of about 1892-93, showing the Chain Pier framed by the substructure of the Palace Pier.

A view of the Palace Pier Theatre in 1902. Note the woman on the left looking into a penny slot machine.

The winter garden of the Palace Pier in about 1918. The winter garden was added close to the shore end in 1910-11. Its latticed ironwork interior was electrically lit from the start. The building still survives, but is now the Palace of Fun amusement arcade.

The Palace Pier photographed at night in the 1920s. The clock tower of the Aquarium can be seen on the left.

The Palace Pier and Aquarium, probably on an August Bank Holiday weekend, c.1925. Between 1927 and 1929 the Aquarium was reconstructed and the distinctive clock tower, seen here on the left, was removed and replaced by a pair of square kiosks with pagoda-style roofs. The pier entrance was altered in 1930, but here the original three ironwork arches are still extant. The banners give some idea of the range of activities and entertainment to which the pier played host. Afternoon and evening concerts were held every Sunday; there was open-air dancing every evening; and for the Bank Holiday weekend, a grand gala and carnival culminated in a firework display. In addition, there was the theatre, then performing *The Blue Train*, and visible beyond it the paddle steamers offered trips along the coast.

Young children enjoying the slide and other amusements on the Palace Pier in 1935. The notice behind sternly reminds visitors that the 'Amusement devices are for the use of young children only'. The building in the background was the pier head pavilion referred to in the title of the original developers of the pier, the Brighton Marine Palace and Pier Company. A large Oriental-looking structure with minarets, the pavilion originally contained a concert hall along with dining, smoking and reading rooms, but it was reformed as a theatre and café in 1910-11. It was demolished in 1986. The pier was at the peak of its popularity in the period either side of World War Two, with two million visitors in 1939.

Madeira Drive looking west, *c.*1895. This was a popular promenade even before Madeira Terrace was added in stages during the 1890s. The first section to the east of Royal Crescent was completed by 1890 and this photograph may have been taken from the point where it ended.

The Madeira Terrace and lift in the mid-1920s. It provides an interesting contrast with the earlier 19th-century view of Madeira Drive. The erection of the Banjo Groynes in 1877 led to land being reclaimed as shingle built up. In 1899 this area was laid out with gardens and bowling greens and became known as the Madeira Lawns. Here a refreshment kiosk selling ice-cream can be seen, behind which is the temporary stage and seating for Jack Sheppard's entertainers. Beyond this again are a row of bathing machines, soon to be replaced by the bathing chalets standing on the other side of Volk's Railway.

The Madeira Lift was designed by the Borough Engineer, Philip Lockwood, and opened in 1890. It provided a smooth, hydraulically operated, descent from Marine Parade to Madeira Drive. A shelter hall was provided at the base; on either side were panelled rooms where visitors could consult newspapers and obtain refreshments. The lift cage was lined with walnut and decorated with mirrors, gilt panels, and medallions. From eight to 15 people could be carried for a fare of a halfpenny each way. Today, the lift is electrically powered and has none of the original decoration. The exterior, however, still survives, with a domed roof decorated with dolphins and an iron weather vane. The shelter hall is now a café. This photograph was taken soon after the lift's opening.

Madeira Walk, Kemp Town, in about 1910. Madeira Walk is a sheltered promenade which forms part of Madeira Terrace. Built between 1890-97 to the designs of Philip Lockwood, the terrace stretched from the Aquarium to Duke's Mound, a distance of 2,837ft. Much of the cast-iron is embellished with Oriental motifs inspired by the Royal Pavilion.

Marine Parade c.1870 during the building of the Aquarium. The entrance to the Chain Pier esplanade has already gone and work has started on the new attraction. In the background the West Pier, opened only four years earlier, can be seen. The wooden rails on the left were to be replaced by iron railings in 1880. Approaching the photographer are two policemen.

A crowded King's Road looking west past the West Pier. The photograph must date from before 1890 when the central windshield was added to the pier. The same view today is much changed. King's Road was not tarmaced until 1907, new ornate lampstands replaced the simple standards in 1893 and the railings fronting the seafront were removed in stages, the final sections going in 1926. The houses on the right, originally known as Queensbury Place, have nearly all been demolished.

Grand Junction Road looking east beyond the partially-built Palace Pier to the Chain Pier. Although work on the Palace Pier began in 1891, financial problems meant that it was not opened to the public until 1899. Grand Junction Road was constructed in 1829 to provide a through route between the King's Road and Marine Parade. Forty-one ornate electric lamp standards were installed along the seafront in 1893. Metal railings replaced wooden ones in 1880, those on the roadside being removed in stages. Note the many umbrellas being carried to protect from the sun, not from the rain. The sun-bathing craze and the desire for a 'healthy' looking tan began to appear only during the Edwardian period when the wealthier middle classes sought out the sun in Continental resorts. The long row of horse-drawn cabs and carriages emphasise how the need to transport visitors around the town provided one of the major areas of employment in late-Victorian Brighton.

The ramp leading down to the beach below Ship Street in the late 1880s. The Aquarium is visible on the left with the Chain Pier on the right and, in between them, Volk's Railway station. The Palace Pier has yet to be built.

King's Road *c.*1895. Today the buildings to the east of the Grand Hotel have all gone, to be replaced by the uninspiring Brighton Centre and Kingswest Boulevard. Prominent amongst these vanished landmarks was Mutton's Hotel and Restaurant which occupied a site between West Street and Russell Street and is clearly visible on the right-hand side of the photograph. Opened by William Sexton Mutton early in Queen Victoria's reign, it finally closed in 1929. Inside, the restaurant was lit by a domed skylight and a large glass chandelier, and the walls were lined with mirrors. Near to the Grand on the western corner of Russell Street stood the Alhambra Opera House and Music Hall which opened in 1888. The flag marks the site of Bolla and Biucchi's Restaurant, Dining and Tea Saloons.

A crowded King's Road opposite the Metropole in 1935.

The crowded boating pool soon after its opening in 1925. Behind stands the West Pier. The attractive structure in the centre is the concert hall, added to the pier in 1916, and beyond this the pier theatre, erected in 1893. The boating pool and garden areas beyond the West Pier were developed in 1925 as part of a general refurbishment programme along the seafront.

A late-1920s view of the boating lake and sunken garden looking west towards the birdcage bandstand.

King's Road, *c.*1932. The distinctive building on the right is the Norfolk Hotel. The motor speedway site which is up for sale was about to be covered by the controversial Embassy Court development. Embassy Court's height, horizontal emphasis, and the use of continuous concrete spandrels creates an unfortunate visual contrast. Fortunately, plans to redevelop Brighton's seafront in like style were not implemented. Note the 'Stop-Me-and-Buy-One' ice-cream seller. A tub or a 'choc bar' cost 4d.

The view from the birdcage bandstand looking west over the western lawns towards the Hove boundary in the late 1920s. The bandstand was built in 1884 as part of a series of improvements to the western esplanade, including the provision of grassed enclosures, flower beds and covered shelters. The seafront gardens were laid out in 1925 to the design of the new Superintendent of Parks and Gardens, Mr B.H.Maclaren, following complaints about the dreary and unattractive nature of much of the seafront. Maclaren added paved walkways, flower beds, lawns and a children's paddling pool. The long, low building on the far right is the former Brunswick Baths, demolished in 1934 when Embassy Court was controversially built on this sensitive site adjacent to Brunswick Terrace.

The beach looking east towards the Chain Pier, *c*.1875. This was a ladies only bathing beach as can be seen from the row of ladies bathing machines. On the far left the Aquarium, opened in 1872, can just be glimpsed but the Palace Pier was not begun until 1890. Note also the wooden groynes.

A crowded beach by the West Pier in the mid-1880s. The Metropole has yet to be built.

A row of ladies' bathing machines by the West Pier *c.*1895. The machines were licensed by the Corporation; by 1874 there were 14 different sites with over 340 machines. Gentlemen were charged 6d per half hour and ladies 9d.

Dalton's mixed bathing beach opposite the Aquarium *c.*1922. By this date bathing machines were rapidly going out of favour. These wooden changing rooms on wheels, drawn into the sea by horses, and from which the bather could then descend, had first appeared in the 18th century. Their first recorded use is at Scarborough in 1735 but they soon caught on and were in use at Brighton before 1750. They were intended, in the words of the local bye-laws of 1874, to 'prevent any indecent exposure of the person of the bather'.

Bathing tents and huts on the front near the Bedford Hotel. As the mobile bathing machines fell from grace, they were replaced by static beach huts and by canvas bathing tents hired for the day.

A crowded beach in the late 1890s. The wooden benches were the forerunners of the deckchair and cost 1d to use.

Building sandcastles on the beach has been a tradition since middle-class Victorians first 'invented' the family seaside holiday. The railway brought growing numbers of middle class families to the town boosted by the railway's early acceptance that children under 12 travelled half price. Although this card purports to be at Brighton, the sand and beach profile suggests it probably was not. The card appears to be an advertising stunt for the magazine *Answers*. The image would have been overprinted with different locations as necessary.

An Edwardian family pose on a groyne.

A Victorian family pose on the beach below the Old Ship Hotel. The coming of the railway, allied with social changes which allowed people with more disposable income to enjoy their time off from work, saw the popularity of family-based seaside holidays grow throughout the 19th century.

The West Pier seen from the beach *c.*1900. The beach is cluttered with fishing and pleasure boats while the rows of wooden seats fulfilled the role of modern deckchairs. The photograph shows the landing stage and pier head added to the pier in 1893. The central concert hall was not added until 1916.

A crowded post-war beach in early 1946. During the war, a section of the Palace Pier was removed to prevent enemy landing. It was not until later in 1946 that the pier was restored.

Children enjoy the paddling pool, located on the seafront in front of the Metropole Hotel, in July 1947.

Typical British holiday weather on a late 1940s Bank Holiday as two young women shelter under towels by the seafront arches.

A row of goat carts, horse-drawn cabs and a flower seller on the King's Road in the early 1890s. At this stage the road was still gas lit; electric lights were introduced into King's Road in September 1893.

Children's donkey rides along the seafront were part of the Victorian creation of the family seaside holiday. Donkeys had been introduced
to the seaside towards the end of the 18th century, when they were ridden by ladies along the beach and cliffs. As Victorian families

came to the seaside, the donkey ride became a popular children's pleasure. This photograph, dating from the early 1930s, shows a group near the Hove boundary. In the background the Peace Statue straddles the boundary between Brighton and Hove.

Mrs Betty Smith (then aged three years) in a goat cart in Regency Square in 1907. Her family were on holiday from London. There is evidence of goat carts in Brighton by 1833. They were quite expensive to hire, costing one shilling for an hour by the mid-19th century.

A vendor and his donkeys in front of Brunswick Terrace in the 1890s.

The *Skylark* in front of the West Pier. The photograph dates from just prior to 1890 when the central windshield was added to the pier. The *Skylark* was one of several boats which took parties of trippers for an hour's sail for one shilling. Many fishermen found the lure of pleasure boating for visitors more appealing than the rigours of fishing. Captain Fred Collins was the most famous example, taking to offering trips on his boat *Skylark* in about 1883. He came to operate a fleet of '*Skylarks*' from the beach near West Street. Captain Collins died in 1912, but his boats are frequently to be seen in contemporary views of the beach.

The *Robert Raikes* lifeboat and crew, probably taken in about 1870. From left to right the crew were identified as follows: Bassett, John Taylor, Harry Mayers, unknown, George Self (second cox), Hummy Downes, Tom Atherall (coxswain), A.H.Sutherland, Bill Baker, Marsh Mayers. Lying on the beach are Tom Harman and Tom Bassett. Standing in the white cap is the Honorary Secretary of the Brighton branch of the Royal National Lifeboat Institution. The RNLI were not the first lifeboat providers in the town. A boat was operated adjacent to the Chain Pier from 1825, but it was not until 1 October 1867 that this boat was installed in a new boathouse in front of the Bedford Hotel. Part of the funding for the new boat came from pennies raised by Sunday School children in Brighton and London, in honour of which the boat was named after the founder of the Sunday School Movement. In 1874 the boat was replaced by another of the same name, which in turn lasted only until 1879. RNLI boats were stationed in Brighton from 1858 until 1931.

The crew of the paddle steamer, *Brighton Queen*, photographed while the boat was moored at the landing stage on the end of the West Pier. P. & A. Campbell's two pleasure steamers, the *Glen Rosa* and the *Brighton Queen* made trips along the coast to other seaside resorts such as Eastbourne, Hastings, Bournemouth, Ventnor and Cowes. In high summer the *Brighton Queen* travelled to Boulogne three times a week. Launched in 1897, she was chartered as a minesweeper at the outbreak of war and was sunk in October 1915 after hitting a mine off the Belgian coast.

The *Devonia* paddle steamer approaches the West Pier landing stage in the 1930s. She spent World War One as a minesweeper and the inter-war years as a pleasure steamer. At Dunkirk in 1940 she was badly damaged, beached, and then used by the Germans as a canteen ship.

A small crowd have gathered in the spring sunshine to watch a group of what at the time were called 'Nigger Minstrels' perform on the lower esplanade near the Birdcage bandstand in May 1890. The quality of such beach-based entertainers was often very dubious. An American visitor commented: 'The Englishman at the sea shore expects his amusements to be brought to his very door . . .(he) sits on the beach, he wants his various entertainments to march by him on the sands, and he will accept the crudest apology in the entertainment line . . .A falsetto-voiced costermonger — (and) a badly trained (banjo) will afford him unutterable delight for a summer.'
This area of gardens and walks was laid out as part of a series of improvements in 1884 which included the erection of the bandstand.

A group of 'blacked-up' minstrels performed outside the Metropole. Such cheap street entertainment was often of poor quality and was the subject of protest from middle-class visitors and residents alike. The photograph is one of a series taken in Brighton in May 1890 by George Henderson.

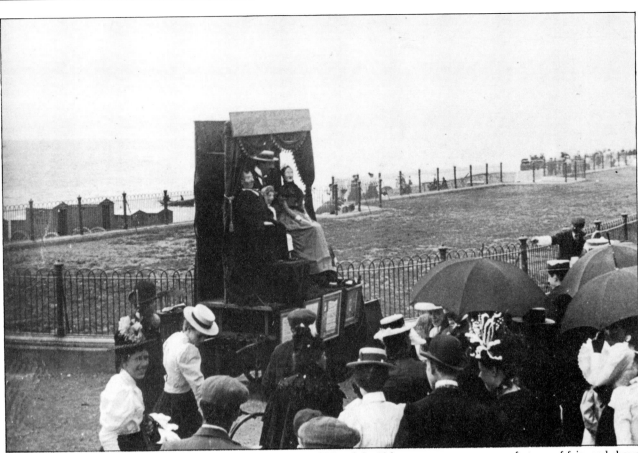

Zeidler's clockwork automata on the beach, late 1890s. From the middle of the 18th century, automata were features of fairs and shows in London. They evidently featured as seafront entertainment in Brighton at the turn of the century.

A street organ performs on the lower esplanade in the late 1890s.

During the 19th century, popular beach entertainment was cheap and cheerful. From the 1840s, simple musical entertainment on the seafront was provided by the 'blacked-up' troupes of 'Nigger Minstrels' but their pre-eminence was challenged in 1891 when Clifford Essex introduced the Pierrots from France. In their distinctive costumes they provided a more refined form of seaside entertainment and were found in most resorts until World War Two. Dressed in traditional Pierrot costume, with large pom-poms and conical hats, they performed sketches, songs and dances up to three or four times a day on small temporary stages erected on the beach or, as in this case, on the Palace Pier. Frequently performers would begin dressed in Pierrot and Pierrette costumes; the men would then change halfway through into straw boaters, blazers or brightly-coloured 'comic' suits. This picture, by Boucher of Brighton, dates from the 1890s.

The Palace Pier Follies in the 1920s. They performed three times daily and twice on Saturdays.

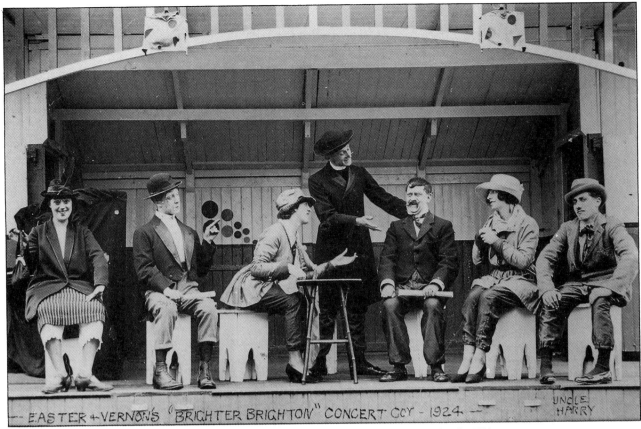

Easter and Vernon's 'Brighter Brighton' Concert Pary performing in 1924.

Punch and Judy on the West Pier
in May 1947.

The Aquarium terrace bandstand in the 1930s. This was added to the Sun Terrace when it was extended eastwards over a colonnade of shops in the reconstruction of 1927-29. The Sun Terrace is now occupied by a small fun fair.

Enjoying the penny-in-the-slot machines on the pier in the late 1920s. These cheap machines appeared in the latter part of the 19th century as part of the trend towards cheap, informal entertainment aimed at a working-class market. They proved very popular in their various forms, whether mechanical automata, or displaying moving pictures often of a risqué nature. Indeed there were campaigns to control indecent mutoscopes or 'what the butler saw' machines.

There were many amusement arcades and stalls offering cheap entertainment for visitors. The site of this rifle range is unidentified. The photograph was one of a series taken by a visiting temperance preacher one Sunday in 1921 to illustrate how the Sabbath was being abused by local tradesmen.

A wooden model of the Edward VII 'Peace' Memorial at the Brighton and Hove boundary. The model was erected in about 1911. The finished monument, designed by Newbury Trent in a competition, was installed in October 1912. Although called a 'Peace' memorial, because the monument takes the form of an angel of peace holding an orb and olive branch, the statue in fact celebrates the reign of Edward VII.

The Undercliff Walk, café, shelter and subway at Saltdean in 1935. In 1928, Rottingdean parish was absorbed by Brighton and in order to protect the coastline an impressive sea wall was erected, initially from Black Rock to Rottingdean, and opened in July 1933. It was extended to Saltdean Gap in July 1935. The final short addition to the borough boundary was under construction when this photograph was taken later in the summer of 1935. Much of the work was undertaken by unemployed workers from Brighton and elsewhere.

The fights between rival gangs of Mods and Rockers at Easter 1964 made headlines in the national news media. The Rockers arrived in the town first and proceeded to occupy the front. The Mods strove to drive them off the seafront under a hail of deckchairs and other missiles. Watched by a crowd of some 3,000, the result was hundreds of pounds' worth of damage and a number of arrests.

The Town Hall was built in 1830-32 by Thomas Cooper, architect of the Bedford Hotel and one of the Brighton Town Commissioners. The building is in the Greek Revival style with Doric and Ionic colonnades derived from the Theseion and Erechtheion in Athens. When first built, the Town Hall was close to the market. John Bruce's *History of Brighton* (1834) commented: 'Butchers . . .occasionally convert the classic Ionic into shambles . . .and but for the disgusting addition of the entrails, the visitor would be led to expect . . .a reception of liveried servants, instead of . . .a mob of bluebottles and all the filthy paraphernalia of the slaughter house'.

ildings

Apart from the usual municipal offices, the Town Hall housed the fire station and police station, and, in the basement, 'underground dungeons similar to which criminals convicted of the darkest crimes would not by any British government be permitted to be consigned' (1862). In 1898-99 extensive alterations were undertaken by Francis May. Part of the works involved the filling in of the upper corners. This photograph was taken in about 1897, prior to the alterations.

The Town Hall during the election of 1859. It was only after 1872 that elections were carried out using the secret ballot. Before then votes were cast in public. Here the crowds of top-hatted gentlemen are being observed from the balcony by their wives. Women were not given the vote until 1918 and then only to those over the age of 30. In 1859, Brighton returned two Liberal MPs, Sir George Pechell and William Coningham.

During the elections of 1895 or 1900, the Central Committee Rooms of the Conservative Party candidates Gerald Loder and Bruce Wentworth stood on the corner of Castle Square and Pavilion Buildings. Brighton gained the right to elect two members to Parliament in 1832. For the first 50 years, Brighton returned Liberal MPs but from the 1880s onwards the Conservatives have dominated. The elections of 1895 and 1900 were no different and Loder and Wentworth were returned.

The Sussex County Hospital and General Sea Bathing Infirmary was built to Charles Barry's designs in 1826-28. Barry's building was seven bays wide with a projecting centre and pediment; room was provided for four large and 23 small wards for 80 patients. In 1838, William Hallett added the Victoria wing and in 1840 Herbert Williams designed the Adelaide wing. Further projecting wings were built in 1853, and there have been many subsequent additions. On its opening in 1828, a contemporary wrote that it was 'a building which testifies that amidst the dissipations of the most fashionable watering place in England, the voice of suffering humanity meets . . .a ready ear and an open hand'.

Howell's almshouses, George Street, were built in 1859 (the date on the pedimented frontispiece is incorrect), at the instigation of Charles Howell, son of a well-known lodging-house keeper and stage coach proprietor. Inmates were elected by the donors and subscribers; they had to be 60 or over, and not in receipt of parish poor relief. The almshouses were demolished in about 1985, following a period of neglect.

The Brighton Asylum for the Blind, later known as the Blind School, was founded in 1839. It moved to a site in Eastern Road in 1860 and George Somers Clarke, who also built the Swan Downer School, designed the new building in 1860-61 in an extraordinarily archaeologically correct Venetian Gothic. Indeed, the building looks as if it has been transported from the Grand Canal. The detailing is taken from Ruskin's *Stones of Venice* (1851-53). The carved medallion over the door depicts the angel of mercy teaching the blind whilst at the apex is a carved figure of charity relieving the blind. The school closed in 1952 and was tragically demolished in 1958.

Dr William Moon's house at 104 Queen's Road, at the end of the 19th century. In 1839, at the age of 21, William Moon lost his sight. He invented a simple embossed system which was simpler to use than braille. The first work in Moon type was produced in 1847, the same year that the Moon Society was formed.

Inside the Moon 'factory' embossed books were produced by teams of blind workers. In 1858, after ten years' work, a Moon Bible of 5,000 pages in 60 volumes was produced, and by Dr Moon's death in 1894 over 500 foreign alphabets had been converted to 'Moon'. William Moon's importance to blind people was summed-up in an article in the *Brighton Gazette* in 1873: 'While the names of the inventors of needle guns, torpedoes and other means of wholesale human destruction, are in everybody's mouth, how few could tell the name of the gentleman whose invention has given light to eyes that cannot see, and knowledge and happiness to minds lost in ignorance or buried in misery? It is really no small local honour that the system was developed and perfected in Brighton'.

St Dunstan's Institute for the Blind, Ovingdean Gap, was built between 1937-39 by Francis Lorne of the partnership of Sir John Burnet, Tait and Lorne. It is one of the new buildings in Brighton in the International Modern style, in this case slightly reminiscent of Charles Holden's London Underground stations. The Institute was founded for the rehabilitation of blinded soldiers, sailors, and airmen, and the plan of the building was apparently based on the shape of a biplane to which it was thought residents could relate. This dramatic view of the chapel, taken for the *Brighton Herald* in 1939, shows a splendid sculptured figure of winged victory holding the St Dunstan's badge.

The former Swan Downer Charity School, Dyke Road, built in 1867 in a late German Gothic style by George Somers Clarke. The school, established in 1819, was originally sited in Gardner Street and Windsor Street. The founder, Swan Downer, was a rich Brighton merchant whose will provided for the instruction of 20 poor girls of the parish in needlework, reading and writing. The photograph was taken in 1933; Smithers and Sons brewery is incongruously located to the right. The school closed in 1939. In later years it became a discothèque, a bizarre transformation from its original purpose.

The Royal Pavilion was completed in its present form by John Nash in 1822. The original south gate was built in 1831 but it was demolished in 1851 when it was replaced by two smaller domed Mughal archways 40 yards to the north. These had cast-iron chatris (*ie* umbrella-shaped domes) enclosing lamps and a low iron gate in between. The second south gate was demolished in 1921 and replaced by a much less agreeable, but more archaeologically correct, gate designed by Thomas Tyrwhitt and based on early 16th-century Gujerati prototypes. The gateway was the gift of the people and princes of India and commemorated the Royal Pavilion's use as a hospital for Indian soldiers. This photograph of the second south gate dates from about 1890.

The entrance foyer of the Royal Pavilion, *c.*1905. The vestibule was dominated by the large statue of Captain William Henry George Pechell. The son of one of the local MPs, he served in the 77th Regiment and was killed at the siege of Sebastapol on 3 September 1855 at the age of 25. A subscription was raised to provide a memorial. On the left there is a bust of the charismatic preacher, the Reverend Frederick Robertson, the incumbent of Holy Trinity Church between 1847 and 1853. Immediately to the left of Captain Pechell is a bust of William Seymour, a local magistrate. This was placed in the Pavilion during his lifetime following a public subscription. To the right is the bust of another local worthy, Sir David Scott. The placing of these busts indicates that the entrance hall of the Royal Pavilion was seen as a 'hall of fame' for local notables.

The interior of the Dome in 1934-35 before the major redevelopment of that year. William Porden designed the building as a stables for the Prince of Wales; it was based on the Paris Corn Market. The stables and adjacent riding school were built between 1803-08. There was room for 44 horses with accommodation for the grooms in the first-floor galleries. After the Corporation purchased the Royal Pavilion Estate in 1850, various uses were proposed including a roller-skating rink, but after a few years as cavalry barracks the Dome was converted into a concert hall and re-opened on 24 June 1867. The dramatic Moorish interior was designed by the Borough Surveyor, Philip Lockwood, and included a superb gas chandelier 30ft high and 16ft in diameter, using 1,300 gas jets.

The Corn Exchange in 1873 was the site for a temporary museum display during the visit to Brighton of the British Association for the Advancement of Science. The display cases were then given to Brighton's new museum, soon to open in neighbouring property in Church Street. The Corn Exchange was originally built by William Porden between 1803 and 1808 as the royal riding school. It became known by its present name in 1868 when the weekly corn market moved here from the King and Queen public house. After World War One it was used for functions and exhibitions. In 1934 alterations by Robert Atkinson left the building as it is today.

Brighton's Museum and Library was designed by the Borough Surveyor, Philip Lockwood, and built between 1872-74. The site, in Church Street, had previously been occupied by stables and a coach house for Queen Adelaide. Lockwood created an entrance at the rear of which was a large picture gallery. This opened in January 1873; the Museum and Library followed in 1874. This picture was taken in April 1900 and shows Lockwood's original three-bay building, constructed, as the *Brighton Gazette* commented, in a 'moderate and strictly Moresque character'.

The Museum and Library was greatly extended between 1901-02 when Francis May, Lockwood's successor as Borough Surveyor, developed the site to the west and east. The new lending and reference library were added on the western side (right), and new entrances were provided, not only for the Dome and Corn Exchange, but also for the Library. May's design was in a rather heavy-handed Islamic style. To the east (left), May added new museum galleries. Here the style was directly copied from Lockwood's earlier building. The *Brighton Herald* commented that the buildings added 'yet another to the varieties of Oriental architecture of which the Pavilion estate is in itself quite a museum'. This photograph, by Donovan of Brighton, was taken six days after the official opening of the new buildings on 5 November 1902.

The Picture Gallery of the Brighton Museum in Church Street in the 1890s. Following the purchase of the Royal Pavilion Estate in 1850, a series of art exhibitions held in the Pavilion raised funds to start a municipal art collection. By 1862 a museum, followed by a public library in 1869, had opened in various rooms in the Pavilion. Space was at a premium and new purpose-built facilities were obviously required. In 1871 a series of coach houses, stables and ancillary buildings were converted into a library, museum and picture gallery by the Borough Surveyor, Philip Lockwood. The Picture Gallery was the first part of the new building to be opened in January 1873. The paintings were hung floor to ceiling in the Victorian manner and top-lit through a glass roof.

In 1804, Mrs Fitzherbert, the Prince of Wales' illegal wife, commissioned William Porden to build her a house on the Steine. Porden's design incorporated a wide flight of steps which led to a ground-floor balcony above which was another balcony with a cast-iron surround of lattice form. Mrs Fitzherbert lived in the house until her death in 1837, after which the house went through a succession of owners until 1873 when it was acquired by the Civil and United Services Club. In 1884, after the house's acquisition by the YMCA, J.G.Gibbins remodelled the interior. Further substantial alterations were carried out in 1927 when the exterior was refaced and an extra floor added. This photograph was taken prior to the 1927 alterations.

Marlborough House, Old Steine, started life as a three-storey red brick building constructed in 1765 for Samuel Shergold, proprietor of the Castle Hotel. In 1771 the house was sold to the Duke of Marlborough, after whom it was named. The Duke lived there in considerable style; the *Lewes Journal* commented: ' 'Tis incredible to think what a deal of money His Grace expends there, and the help he is to the poor. We are well assured that he buys half a bullock a time, a whole calf, and his mutton by the carcase, so that, by the over abundance of his tables, the poor have joints given them hardly touch'd'. In 1786 the house was bought by William 'Single Speech' Hamilton, who employed Robert Adam to reface and remodel both the exterior and interior. Adam's elevation consists of five bays, the two outer bays projecting under plain pediments. On the ground floor are two of Adam's variants on the Venetian window: a blank band above the window to make a round arched feature. Some of Adam's characteristic ceilings survive inside.

The Royal Albion Hotel was built on the site of Russell House in 1826. The architect was Amon Henry Wilds. This late 19th-century view shows the original building with a rusticated ground floor and first and second floors with attached Corinthian columns and Corinthian pilasters. The semi-circular shell heads to the attic storey are characteristic of the architect. The western wing immediately to the right of the main block, with giant fluted Ionic columns and Doric pilasters, was added soon afterwards. The Royal Albion rapidly became one of the most fashionable of Brighton hotels. After a period of decline at the end of the 19th century, it entered upon a new lease of life in 1913 when it was purchased by the charismatic Harry Preston, who extensively restored and remodelled the fabric. Since then there have been many further alterations and additions.

The Bedford Hotel, King's Road, was built in 1829 by Thomas Cooper. It was one of the most distinguished buildings in Brighton. The recessed centre had a screen of Ionic columns and, above, two storeys with Grecian motifs. In the 1850s the hotel was the most fashionable in Brighton. Charles Dickens was a regular visitor; he wrote *Dombey and Son* whilst staying there. In 1964, fire ravaged the building and it was subsequently demolished. Its undistinguished successor is by R. Seifert and Partners.

The Norfolk Hotel, rebuilt in 1864-66 by Horatio Goulty in a French Second Empire style, replaced the Norfolk Arms which had existed on the site since 1824. Moorecroft's *Brighton Guide* (1866) considered the hotel to be the most beautiful building in Brighton.

King's Road in about 1890. Prominent on the right is the Queen's Hotel, built in 1846 on the site of the Dolphin Inn. The bow-fronted house to the immediate left of the hotel, and which now forms part of it, was designed by A.H.Wilds in about 1825.

The sun lounge of the Grand Hotel in the 1930s.

The Grand Hotel was built in the Italianate style by the London architect John Whichcord in 1862-64. When built it was the tallest structure in Brighton; contemporary descriptions refer to a 'Cyclopean pile' and the *Pictorial World* (1875) was reminded of 'palaces abroad than of hotels at home'. The interior had coffee rooms for ladies and gentlemen, two conservatories in an exotic oriental style, a library, billiard and smoking room. There were 300 rooms in all. The staircase was decorated with Cupids and bunches of grapes painted in a Raphaelesque manner by Signor Galli of London. The numerous gas brackets were formed as bronze angels carrying flambeaux. The scagliola decoration was executed by R.Warren of London and the carving and modelling was by Adam Gamble of Westminster. The twin towers contained monster water cisterns for the five hydraulic lifts. There were 3,500,000 bricks, 15 miles of wallpaper, six miles of gas pipes, and 12 miles of bell wire. The cost was £150,000. The hotel was severely damaged by a terrorist bomb on 12 October 1984; it has since been meticulously restored.

Markwell's Royal Hotel in about 1880. The hotel was built in 1870 on the site of Sake Deen Mahomed's vapour baths. The foundations incorporated part of the wall of the battery, built by the Board of Ordnance in 1760. Markwell's was absorbed by the nearby Queen's Hotel in 1908.

The Metropole Hotel in about 1896. The hotel was built in 1888-90 to the designs of Alfred Waterhouse. The *British Architect* wrote in 1892: 'It is a wonderful relief to come upon the . . .hotel with its warm colour, picturesque skyline, and variety of light and shade in corbelled balconies and recessed windows and dormers.' The hotel was electrically lit from the start and boasted 300 bedrooms, 44 dressing rooms, and 17 sitting rooms. The roofline was spoilt in 1961 when two additional storeys were added; these necessitated the removal of the central spire and turrets.

This 1915 photograph by Bedford Lemere of the dining room at the Metropole Hotel hints at the lost glories of the once lavish interior. The state suite on the first floor consisted of a drawing room in Louis XVI style, a dining room, and numerous private dining rooms. The dining room was decorated by Maple and Company in a vaguely Renaissance style. The chairs, also by Maple's, boasted the badge of the hotel in beaten gold.

Marine Parade was developed eastwards from the Steine from the 1790s. Many of the houses were refronted by C.A.Busby and A.H.Wilds in the 1820s. With the development of the promenade in 1827-38, the whole area became a fashionable carriage drive which extended from Kemp Town to Brunswick Town. The striking house on the left is now the Lanes Hotel. It was refronted and remodelled in a fashionable Queen Anne style in 1880 by Colonel Robert Edis of the Artists' Rifles. The steep gables and white painted windows and verandahs against a red brick and flint background led Goodhart-Rendel to comment in 1933: 'The house . . .does look as if it meant to have a good time, as if it expected sunshine, and knew how to make the most of it'.

This postcard of Rock Mansion, Lower Rock Gardens, was produced to advertise a boarding house run by Mrs Crockford. Boarding houses provided rooms as well as communal sitting and dining rooms. The street was originally built as Rock Buildings in the 1790s, but the addition of a communal garden led to a change of name. This house was typical of those built in the early 19th century with four storeys, angular bays and a balcony.

The Central National School was founded by Henry Wagner, vicar of Brighton, and designed by two Brighton builders, Stroud and Mew, in a stuccoed Regency Gothic style. It was built in 1829-30 in Church Street at the north end of New Road. The school provided a free education for poor children on Church of England principles. After closure in 1967, the school was tragically demolished in 1971.

The Diocesan Training College for the Mistresses of National Schools was built in Viaduct Road in 1853-54 on land given by William Stanford of Preston. Accommodation was provided for 40 female students, who were required to live lives of monastic seclusion and spartan simplicity. The building was designed in the Gothic style by W.G. & E.Habershon. The symmetrical knapped flint front was extended in 1886 by Scott and Cawthorn. The building still survives as the Brighton Business Centre; it has been shorn of its chimneys and cast-iron railings.

Brighton College was founded in 1845 and moved to its present site in 1849. The aim of the school was 'to provide for the Sons of Noblemen and Gentlemen a sound religious, Classical, Mathematical, and general education'. The earliest buildings, shown here in an engraving, are in flint and Caen stone and are built in a style derived from 'Collegiate' Gothic of the 14th century. They were designed by Sir Gilbert Scott and built between 1848-66. With the demolition of Brills' Baths, this is now the only building by Scott in Brighton and Hove. Goodhart-Rendel commented in 1933: 'Brighton might almost share the boast of a former Dean of Lincoln, who said that his proudest epitaph would be, "He kept Sir Gilbert out"'.

The gatehouse and new classrooms of Brighton College were added by Sir Thomas Graham 'Anglo' Jackson, a pupil of Scott and an old boy of the school, who was appointed architect soon after Scott's death in 1878. The gatehouse dates from 1885-86. The style is a rich Tudor Gothic in brick and terracotta. The latter was used 'to resist the trying climate of the south coast'.

Infants' drill taking place at the Pelham Street Infants' School, *c.*1910. The school was built in 1906 as an annex to the York Place Elementary School. The need for physical exercise was particularly emphasised in board schools. The school was renamed the Fawcett School for Boys and the Margaret Hardy School for Girls and moved to Patcham in the 1960s.

Female students at work in the laboratory at the York Place schools around the turn of the century. The York Place Schools were originally established as Elementary Schools by the Brighton School Board in 1870; 14 years later technical and commercial subjects were added. The introduction of female technical education was a rarity.

In 1875 it was decided to move the School of Art and Science from the Royal Pavilion kitchens to a site on Grand Parade. The new building was designed by the Brighton architect John Gibbins in a style that was described as 'a modern adaptation of the Romanesque'. The foundation stone was laid in June 1876 by Sir Henry Cole, first director of the South Kensington Museum (later the Victoria and Albert Museum), and the school was opened in 1877 by Princess Louise and the Marquess of Lorne. On either side of the façade were two terracotta relief panels which are of interest as they indicate the original function of the building. The Arts were represented by pottery, architecture, sculpture, geometry, building construction and painting; the Sciences had figures symbolic of astronomy, electricity, navigation, microscopy, geology, botany, agriculture and entomology. The panels were designed by Alexander Fisher, headmaster of the school. In 1965, the School of Art and Science was demolished. Le Corbusier was proposed as the architect of the new Faculty of Art and Design; in the event the buildings which now occupy the site were designed by Percy Billington, the Borough Architect, and opened in 1967.

The Municipal Technical College, Richmond Terrace, was built between 1895-98 to the designs of Francis May. It cost £28,000. The aim of the technical college was to provide a 'scientific, technical, commercial, and general education'. Like many of May's buildings, the style is 'Free Renaissance' expressed in red brick and terracotta.

Roedean School is generally recognised as Britain's most famous girls' public school. It was built in 1897-99 to the designs of Sir John Simpson, who used an Arts and Crafts version of the Jacobean style. The 500ft frontage combined both staff and girls' quarters. A chapel was added in 1906, followed by the junior school and sanatorium in 1908, and an art school and library in 1911. The school was founded by the Misses Lawrence; it was initially intended as preparatory school for Newnham College, Cambridge.

In 1768, Dr John Awsiter published *Thoughts on Brighthelmston. Concerning Sea-Bathing and Drinking Sea Water with some directions for their use*. The pamphlet praised the use of sea water baths 'for those who are so unhappy as to be invalids'. A year later Awsiter employed the architect Robert Golden to build hot and cold water baths on what is now the south-west side of Pool Valley. The baths consisted of six cold baths, a hot bath, a showering bath and a sweating bath. None was communal as each bath was intended for indivudal use. A shampooing bath, first used by Sake Deen Mahomed, was added later. This had nothing to do with shampooing in its present sense. It was more like a sauna in which the limbs were massaged; a contemporary described it as 'a sort of stewing alive by steam'. Awsiter's baths were subsequently taken over by Wood and then by Creak, who employed George Lynn to add another storey and extend the building southwards. Creak's baths were demolished in 1861 when Brill's baths were extended. This early photograph shows the baths just prior to demolition.

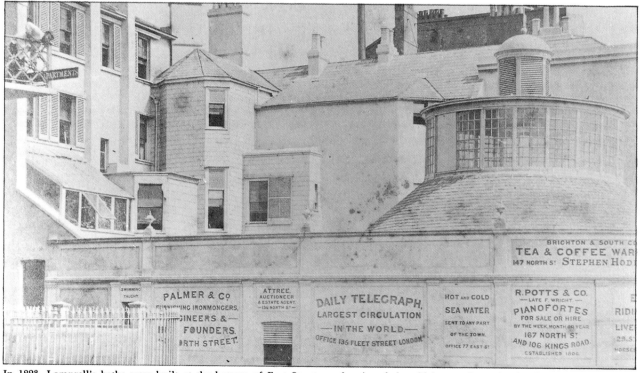

In 1823, Lamprell's baths were built at the bottom of East Street on the site of the old battery in a circular domed building with a glazed lantern surmounted by a cupola; the building became known as 'the bunion'. In 1840, Charles Brill took over the concern and in 1858 the baths were remodelled. Four years later Brill opened a new ladies swimming bath.
East Street was a particularly suitable location for hot and cold baths as pipes could readily be laid to pump the sea water. The site was also close to a popular sea bathing area. This photograph was taken about 1855.

In 1869, Charles Brill erected a new gentlemen's swimming bath to the designs of Gilbert Scott. This large red brick building between East Street and Pool Valley had a circular iron dome and lantern surrounded by two tiers of Gothic arcading. The circular swimming bath, 65ft in diameter, was the largest in Europe at the time. Brill's baths were demolished in 1929 to make way for the Savoy (now Cannon) cinema.

The clock tower was commissioned in 1887 by John Willing, an advertising magnate, to celebrate Queen Victoria's Golden Jubilee. It was built, to the designs of John Johnson, in 1888. The style is a rather mongrel Victorian baroque. On the base are four mosaic portraits of the Royal Family: Prince Albert, Queen Victoria, Edward, Prince of Wales, and Princess Alexandra. Above these are four carved boats pointing to the sea, the station, Hove and Kemp Town. Magnus Volk designed an ingenious mechanism by which a hydraulically operated gilt copper time ball rose up the 16ft mast and fell on the hour. The ball was activated by an electrical signal from Greenwich. Unsurprisingly, it functioned for only a few years.

Churches

St Nicholas' Church, from a watercolour by Frederick Earp, 1853. Earp's view shows the ancient parish church of Brighton prior to R.C.Carpenter's savage restoration of 1853-54. The steps to the right of the south porch led to 18th-century galleries, which were placed on every side of the church; they were lit by the dormer windows in the roof. The interior had box-pews arranged round the font. After Carpenter's restoration, which was carried out as a memorial to the Duke of Wellington who had worshipped in the church as a boy, the church was all but rebuilt. All that survives today from the 14th-century building, is the tower, nave arcades, chancel arch, screen, and font. It is ironic that a 'restoration' carried out in the Duke of Wellington's name should have destroyed all the features of the church with which he was familiar.

The interior of St Peter's Church, Preston, in about 1880. St Peter's is an excellent example of a 13th-century Sussex church, but it was severely restored in 1872 by James Woodman. The medieval wall paintings were discovered in 1830 but were severely damaged by fire in 1906. The church is now in the care of the Redundant Churches Fund.

The chancel of St Peter's, Preston, in about 1880. This fascinating view dates from soon after Ewan Christian's restoration of the chancel in 1878. The very pretty decorative stencilling, part of which survives, is presumably by him. The altar is in the form of a tomb chest which dates from 1515; it originally stood against the north wall. Above is a painting of the Deposition of Christ, probably by N.Westlake. It was unfortunately moved in 1907 and now hangs on the south wall of the nave. The Reverend Gerald Moor, writing in 1907, described the picture as 'most painful'.

The Chapel Royal, Prince's Place, was built in 1793-95 by Thomas Saunders of London for the Reverend Thomas Hudson, who hoped to attract the Prince of Wales. However, the Prince attended only infrequently and he left the chapel for good after an objectionable sermon was preached from the text 'Thou art the man'. The last member of the Royal Family to attend the chapel was Princess Augusta, who frequented it until her death in 1840. This photograph shows the chapel before its remodelling by Sir Arthur Blomfield in 1876-82. The simple classical building is surmounted by a Coade stone coat of arms (which still survives); the glazed lantern was added in 1848 to the designs of G.Lynn of Brighton.

The Chapel Royal after Sir Arthur Blomfield's remodelling. Blomfield's work was carried out in stages between 1876-82; the clock tower and new entrances came last. The style is Free Renaissance, carried out in red brick and terracotta.

Duke Street and Holy Trinity Church before 1867. Duke Street was developed in the early 18th century when it was known as Cragg's Lane. It was a narrow street only 17ft wide. In 1817, Trinity Chapel was built by Amon Wilds for Thomas Read Kemp, the developer of Kemp Town, for his own personal dissenting sect, but Kemp had political ambitions and so returned to the Church of England. In 1825 he sold the chapel to the Reverend Robert Anderson and his brother, who formed the Anglican Holy Trinity Church. Reputedly using the architect Charles Barry, who had recently designed St Peter's Church and the Sussex County Hospital and was later to become famous for the Houses of Parliament, they enlarged and redesigned the chapel. In 1867, as part of a road widening scheme, the houses abutting the church in Duke Street which contained the vestry and Sunday Schools were demolished, exposing the southern façade of Holy Trinity. As compensation the church was given land at the rear on which it built a new chancel and vestries. In 1885-87, Somers Clarke rebuilt the east (liturgical west) end in a rather thin Gothic style. The building remained in use until Christmas 1985.

Christ Church Unitarian Chapel, New Road, was built in 1820 to the designs of A.H.Wilds; the imposing Greek Doric portico is modelled on the Temple of Theseus in Athens. The bow-fronted house to the right, with a later shop front, is also probably by Wilds. It has a particuarly splendid iron canopied balcony.

The Countess of Huntingdon's Chapel, North Street, in 1869. This fascinating photograph shows the chapel before it was rebuilt in 1871. Selina, Countess of Huntingdon, came to Brighton in 1755 owing to the illness of her youngest son. An early convert to Methodism, she achieved notoriety by selling some of her jewels in order to enlarge a chapel at the back of her house in North Street in 1766. The building was the first of a group of chapels known as the 'Countess of Huntingdon's Connexion'. The chapel was rebuilt in 1774, enlarged in 1822-23, and enlarged again in 1842. The Ionic temple front must date from 1822-23. The *Brighton Times* commented in 1863: 'A pediment, with no portico beneath, rests on four fluted Ionic columns, which yet are not quite columns . . .They look as if they were grown out of the wall whereunto they still adhere, and as if they were afraid to advance any further.' The chapel was demolished in 1870, when a new church was built on the site.

St George's Church, Kemp Town, was built in 1824-25 by C.A.Busby for Thomas Read Kemp. The church is in a Greek Revival style and consists of a yellow brick box with two tiers of windows under a cornice. The west front has recessed giant Ionic columns between pilasters topped by a square tower and cupola. The inside retains its galleries. St George's was built as a proprietary chapel for the Kemp Town estate. Pews or 'sittings' were allocated according to the number of shares in the new building bought by each shareholder or 'proprietor'. The pews then became the property of the shareholder and could be rented or sold. The system was particularly prevalent in the coastal towns of Sussex. It was regarded with horror by later Victorian churchmen.

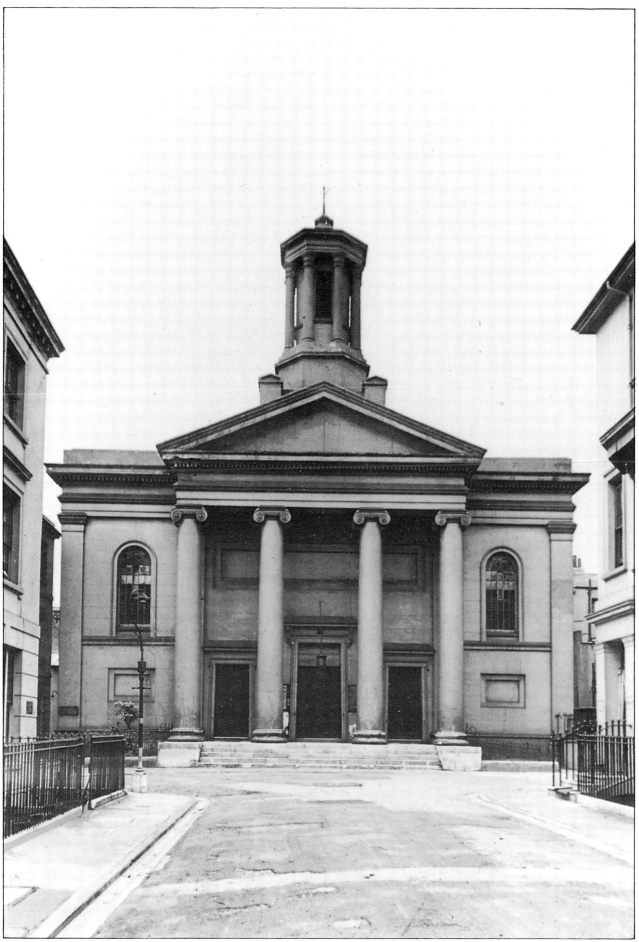

St Margaret's Church, Cannon Place, was built in 1824, probably by the Brighton architect C.A.Busby, for Barnard Gregory, editor of the *Brighton Gazette*, who, astonishingly, named the church after his wife. As with many early 19th-century churches, St Margaret's was built as a speculation; the income to support the curate and provide a profit for Gregory came from the sale or rental of pews. The west elevation had an impressive Greek Ionic portico which was surmounted by a belfry derived from the Tower of the Winds in Athens. The church was demolished in 1959.

The interior of St Margaret's Church, c.1940. Busby's inventiveness can be seen in the way he has married the dome to the square nave. The galleries carry cast-iron foliate and Corinthian capitals. The *Brighton Gazette* commented in 1875 that the church was 'stamped with the Protestant seal of the Georgian era, its architecture (being) that of the meeting house style'.

The Hanover Chapel, Queen's Road, was built in 1824 for the Rev James Edwards of Petworth. The Presbyterians took it over in 1844 and remained until 1972. It now forms part of the Brighthelm Centre. The façade is distinguished by baseless Roman Doric porches, end window bays with Doric pilasters, and recessed round headed windows. It may have been designed by Thomas Cooper.

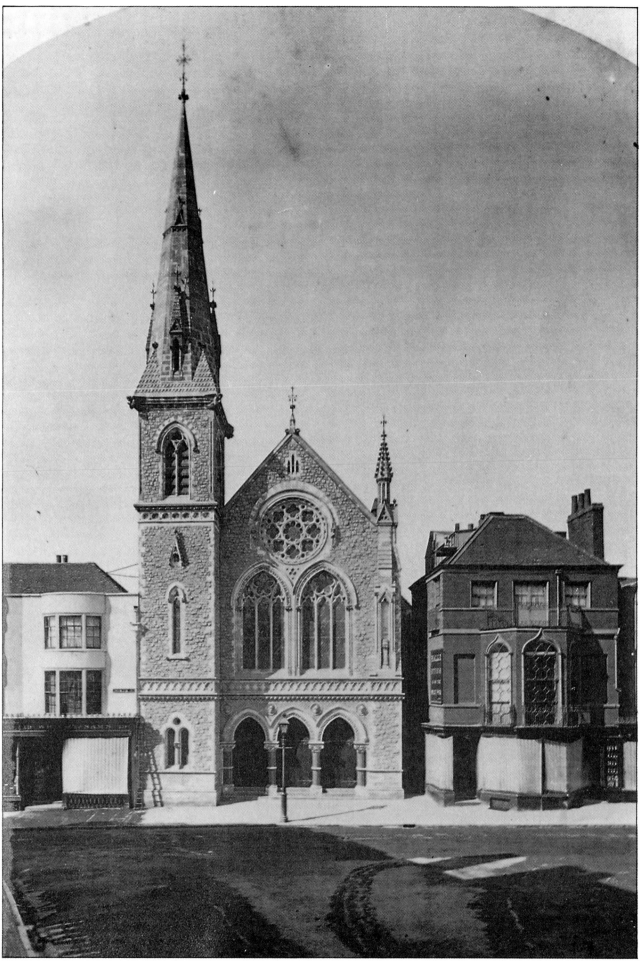

The Countess of Huntingdon's Church, North Street, in about 1876. This photograph, by Boucher of Brighton, shows the newly rebuilt church soon after completion in 1871. The architect was John Wimble of Brighton. To the right is a house with a delightful ogee arched 'Gothick' bay window. The church was tragically demolished in 1972.

St Peter's Church is one of the finest early Gothic Revival Commissioners' churches in the country. It was built between 1824-28 by Charles (later Sir Charles) Barry as a chapel of ease to the parich church of St Nicholas. The style, as was usual at the time, is Perpendicular Gothic but, unlike most Commissioners' churches, it was expensive (£20,365) because it was built of Portland stone instead of stucco, and because Barry designed an ambitious tower to provide a grand termination to the north end of the Steyne. The lower part of the tower has a buttressed screen with flying buttresses at the four corners. This allowed Barry to provide three enormously high entrances which otherwise would have rendered the structure unstable. The interior, however, was much less inventive. In essence it was a large Georgian preaching house tricked out with Gothic detail. There were north, south and west galleries, box pews, a pair of pulpits, one for the service, and one for the sermon, and no distinct chancel. A new chancel was built in 1898-1906 to the designs of Somers Clarke and J.T.Micklethwaite. In 1873, St Peter's became the parish church of Brighton.

St Paul's Church viewed from Little Russell Street in about 1950. This part of Brighton has been comprehensively redeveloped but St Paul's Church still dominates the area. It was built by R.C.Carpenter in 1846-48. The octagonal lantern was added by Carpenter's son, R.H.Carpenter, in 1874-75. The church was the first in Brighton to be built on the principles laid down by the Cambridge Camden Society. The *Ecclesiologist* wrote in 1846: 'At last Brighton is to have its part in the revival of church architecture, and its hideous chapels are to be shamed by a real church.'

St Stephen's Church, Montpelier Place, is, historically, one of the most interesting buildings in Brighton. The main body of the church was originally the ballroom of the Castle Inn Assembly Rooms, Castle Square. The ballroom was added to the Castle Inn in *c.*1776; the architect was John Crunden. In 1822, the Castle Inn was bought by George IV, who demolished the building but converted the ballroom into a private chapel with seating for 400. Apart from members of the King's household, admission was by ticket signed by the vicar of Brighton. When the Royal Pavilion was acquired by the town in 1850, the Royal Chapel, as a consecrated building, was claimed by the Church Commissioners. It was then moved to Montpelier Place in 1851, provided with a classical front by Cheesman of Brighton, and opened as St Stephen's Church. Since then the church has undergone various modifications, most notably in 1889 when Arthur Blomfield remodelled the interior. Features from the ballroom still survive, however, most notably the fluted columns which support a delicate Adamesque neo-classical cornice. The church now houses a day centre for the homeless.

The Union Congregational Church, Queen's Square, was built in an Early English style in 1853-54 to the designs of James and Brown. A south-west tower was projected but never built; the stump can be seen in this picture taken for the *Brighton Herald* in 1935. In 1867 the church was enlarged and the interior remodelled by Mr Poulton of Reading, and in 1884 the exterior was refaced. The church was sadly closed in 1983 and demolished a year later. The site is now occupied by the inevitable shops and offices.

St Michael and All Angels Church, Victoria Road, was designed by G.F.Bodley for the Reverend Charles Beanlands and built between 1861-62. It was the first brick-built church in Brighton, and shows the influence of G.E.Street and William Butterfield on the young architect. In later life Bodley dismissed it as 'a boyish, antagonistic effort'. The interior contains superb Morris and Company stained glass. The early services in the church were the most ritualistically advanced in Brighton. This photograph, taken in about 1870, shows the church from the west.

The elaborate services at St Michael's Church attracted capacity congregations and it soon became clear the church was too small. In 1868, William Burges was asked to draw up plans to enlarge the church. Lack of money and the opposition of the vicar of Brighton, Henry Wagner, unfortunately prevented the execution of Burges' designs until 1893-95. Burges died in 1881 and John Chapple, Burges' office manager, was the executant architect. Chapple considerably modified his master's plans, but the bones of Burges' designs survived. Bodley's original church became the south aisle, and a vast nave and chancel, of cathedral dimensions, were added. the style is Northern French Gothic of the 13th century. The additions can be seen to the right of Bodley's church in this 1940s photograph.

The Dials Congregational Church, Dyke Road, was built in 1870-71 by Thomas Simpson of Brighton in a Romanesque and Transitional style. The church boasted a horseshoe-shaped auditorium and a 150ft high Rhenish clock tower. The grandiose building well symbolised the confidence of 19th-century congregationalism. The photograph was taken in 1969, prior to the church's demolition in 1972.

St Bartholomew's Church, Ann Street, has been called the Cathedral of Brighton Anglo-Catholicism. It was built between 1872-74 by the local architect Edmund Scott for Father Wagner of Brighton, the fervent High Church sacramentalist. The church is four feet higher than Westminster Abbey; it is probably the highest parish church in the country. The unique and breathtaking interior has enormously high brick walls admirably set-off by the opulent furnishings designed by Henry Wilson between 1895-1908. The massive neo-Byzantine baldachino is particularly striking. John Betjeman once imagined the clergy entering on elephants.

St Bartholomew's Church in about 1900. The picture illustrates the way in which the church dominated the working-class area in which it was built. The elevation owes little to precedent and reflects the eclecticism and more original treatment of medieval sources current in Victorian architecture from the 1850s. The vast height may owe something to James Brooks' contemporary work in London, as well as Spanish Catalan architecture and 13th-century Italian friars' churches. It was criticised at the time it was completed in 1874 as resembling a Noah's Ark or monster cheese warehouse. The small houses and workshops have all been demolished.

St Martin's Church, Brighton, was designed by Somers Clarke in 1872-75 as a memorial to Henry Wagner, vicar of Brighton, who died in 1870. The exterior of the church is in a severe Early English style whilst the magnificent interior boasts fittings designed by the architect; these include the vast Spanish-inspired reredos which was constructed in Germany and carved by J.E.Knox. The figures were carved by Joseph Mayr of Oberammergau, and the painting was by H.Ellis Wooldridge. The roof is painted with 70 panels representing the expansion of the Anglican communion; colonial sees are painted on one side, and American sees on the other. The church was the first in the country to be provided with a wood block parquet floor.

The synagogue in Middle Street was built to the designs of the Brighton architect Thomas Lainson in 1874-75. The Byzantine/Romanesque façade has round arched windows with voussoirs of blue and red tiles. The sumptuous interior, which owes much to the munificence of the Sassoon family, has galleries raised on marble columns with capitals carved with fruits mentioned in the Old Testament. Antony Dale has described the interior of the synagogue as not only the finest in Britain, but amongst the most splendid in Europe.

St Mary's Church, St James' Street, was rebuilt in 1877-79 by Sir William Emerson in a French Gothic style. Emerson, a pupil of William Burges, worked primarily in India where he became a master of Anglo-Indian Gothic; he designed little of importance in England and this church is his most substantial work. The interior is distinguished by some vaulting in the manner of J.L.Pearson, and excellent stained glass by Clayton and Bell.

Housing

The west side of the Old Steine, *c*.1885. The white building with two large, round-headed windows is Marlborough House. Originally built in 1765, the house was in use as offices by the Brighton School Board from 1870. To the right is Steine House, originally built in 1804 by William Porden for Mrs Fitzherbert, but since 1884 the YMCA has occupied the building. In the foreground is the Victoria Fountain erected in 1846 by public subscription to celebrate the Queen's 27th birthday.

The Old Steine in about 1890. The name 'Steine' possibly derives from a Flemish word meaning a stone. The area was originally used by fishermen for drying their nets but by the 1750s the Steine was being used as a fashionable promenade. In 1776 wooden railings were erected and the area was turfed; by the 1780s all activities apart from promenading were forbidden. In 1823, an iron fence was erected which survived until 1921 when it was replaced by a dwarf fence. The photograph shows the Royal Pavilion to the north; the large block of buildings immediately to the south replaced the Castle Hotel, which was demolished in 1823. They in turn were demolished in 1930. To the east are a group of late 18th-century houses, many of which were refronted in the early 19th century. In the centre of the Steine is the Victoria Fountain, designed in 1846 by Amon Henry Wilds.

These two houses, 3 and 4 Pavilion Parade, were built in the late 1790s. They are of great interest because, unlike the great majority of Brighton's 18th-century houses, they were not refronted in the 1820s. The fronts retain the original tarred (now painted) cobbles, with painted brick dressings and quoins. The windows of the left-hand house have unfortunately had their original glazing bars replaced by Victorian plate glass.

Numbers 3-4 Old Steine were built in 1790 at right-angles to North Parade. They formed part of a group of four houses which, on the occasion of one of the Prince of Wales' visits to the town, were painted in the Whig colours of blue and buff in order to please the Prince. They were ever afterwards known as 'the Blues and Buffs'. Two houses (numbers 1 and 2 Old Steine) were demolished in 1928, but 3 and 4 still survive. The cobbled house has an unaltered vernacular façade, but number 4 was refronted in about 1820. The photograph was taken in about 1948.

Royal Crescent is important in the history of Brighton for two reasons: it was the first terrace built facing the sea; and it was the most ambitious housing development of its time. The crescent was built as a speculation by J.B.Otto, a West Indian plantation owner. Building started in 1798, but owing to Otto's financial problems, it was not completed until 1807. The generous layout of the crescent is due to the fact that the land was owned by only one person. The houses are of vernacular construction, with timber-framed carcasses and brick infill faced with glazed mathematical tiles. The great majority have canted bays, and neo-classical doorcases which occasionally differ in their construction. The architect is unknown.

Regency Square was developed between 1818-28 by the landowner J.F.Hanson on a site, known as Belle Vue Field, which had been used for fairs and military reviews. The plots were let on building leases and builders were compelled to erect uniform façades, possibly to the designs of Amon Wilds and Amon Henry Wilds. The ground and first floors were to be stucco rendered, while the upper storeys were to be of yellow brick with stone dressings. The majority of the houses had bow fronts with attractive canopies, many of which have subsequently been removed. This photograph, of about 1890, was taken when the houses were still in private ownership. Today, many have been converted into flats or hotels. An underground car park was constructed in 1969.

Gothic House, later known as The Priory or Priory Lodge, was built between 1822-25 to the designs of A.H.Wilds and C.A.Busby. It may have been their only executed design in the Regnecy Gothic idiom and, taken together with the nearby Western Pavilion (*qv*), nicely illustrates the stylistic eclecticism of the Regency period. The house has been much altered: in 1880 the north façade was rebuilt in a simplified Gothic style by W.H.Stevens, and in 1898 much of the ground floor was converted into a shop for Sharmar's drapery emporium. Gothic House is now occupied by Debenham's store. This photograph dates from about 1870.

An Edwardian view of Norfolk Square, looking north of Western Road. The square was developed in the 1820s. The three and four-storeyed bow-fronted houses with first-floor balconies are very typical of Regency house design in Brighton.

Wykeham Terrace was built from 1827-30 in a charming Regency Gothic style. The architect may have been either A.H.Wilds or Henry Mew. Between 1855-1912 numbers 1-5 and 8-11 housed part of what became St Mary's Home for female penitents, founded by the Reverend George Wagner for the reformation of prostitutes. Wagner, a nephew of Henry Wagner, vicar of Brighton, died aged 42 in Malta. He has been described as 'a bronchitic missionary to the fallen women of Brighton'.

The Western Pavilion, Western Terrace, was built probably in the late 1820s or early 1830s by A.H.Wilds for his own use. The onion dome (which contains a large bathroom), and Hindu details, provoked Pevsner to describe the building as 'The Royal Pavilion's baby brother'. Wilds later moved to the nearby Gothic House (Priory Lodge).

Gloucester Place photographed in 1899. These early 19th-century houses no longer survive and the front gardens were removed for road widening soon after the picture was taken. Two of the houses in the picture are evidently being re-stuccoed. The site is now occupied by the Astoria Cinema.

This photograph of Ship Street and Prince Albert Street by Boucher of Brighton was taken in about 1872. It shows an attractive group of late 18th and early 19th-century houses. Note the wooden slatted Venetian blinds in the windows of the house on the left. Today, the houses still survive, but they have been altered. The fine doorcase on the house on the left has gone; the bow windows are now canted on the house next door; and the building on the far left of the picture has been replaced.

Oriental Place was initially conceived as part of a scheme which would have included an oriental garden and conservatory, known as the Athenaeum. The Athenaeum, the brain-child of Henry Phillips, was to be a triple-domed building which would have housed a collection of tropical plants, a library, school, and museum. Although lack of financial support caused the scheme to be abandoned, Oriental Place was half-complete by the time Sir David Scott of Sillwood Park, Berkshire, bought the site. He retained Amon Henry Wilds as architect, and Oriental Place was completed in 1827. The terraces are distinguished by features typical of the architect: 'Ammonite' capitals, and semi-circular shell motifs above the first floor windows. The Sillwood Hall Hotel, just visible in this late 19th-century postcard, was built by Wilds as Sir David Scott's own residence. It was originally called Sillwood House and was built on the site of the projected Athenaeum. It is now used as a warehouse.

Sussex Square forms part of the Kemp Town estate developed by Thomas Read Kemp from 1823. The façades of the Sussex Square houses were designed by C.A.Busby and built by A.H.Wilds in 1828, although the interiors had to be completed by the purchasers. Every third house is emphasised by Corinthian pilasters.

Lewes Crescent is a fascinating example of town planning on a major scale. The architect, C.A.Busby, designed the houses in groups of three, with changes in floor level in every group to allow for the slight hill on which they are built; every third house is emphasised by giant pilasters and a forward façade with Tuscan or Doric columns. The façades were completed by 1827-28, although the majority of houses remained empty shells for several years. Lewes Crescent, together with Sussex Square, forms the centrepiece of the Kemp Town estate; the inspiration is from Bath and Nash's terraces around Regent's Park, but there is a signficant variation: instead of looking to the countryside, Kemp's estate faces the sea.

Brunswick Square, Hove, was developed between 1825-28 by Charles Augustin Busby on land owned by the Reverend Thomas Scutt. The square formed part of the massive Brunswick Town development in which Busby envisaged a scheme which would correspond to the western equivalent of Kemp Town. The grand terraces were to be served by shops, a market, an hotel and a chapel. The houses in Brunswick Square are of similar size to those in Kemp Town and Regent's Park, London. They are built in groups of four with unbroken cornices; façades are articulated with giant Ionic columns or Tuscan pilasters. The plan of each house followed the standard first-class London town house; the basement was occupied by servants' rooms, the ground floor had a hall, dining room and morning room, the first floor a drawing room, the second floor houses the bedrooms, while the servants slept in the attic. By the 1930s, however, many of the houses had been divided up into poor flats and demolition was seriously considered in 1945. The resulting outcry led to the foundation of the Regency Society of Brighton and Hove, and it is largely due to their tireless campaigning that Brunswick Town survives today.

Portland Place was built between 1824-28 to the designs of C.A.Busby. The speculating landowner, Major Villeroy Russell, was evidently influenced by Busby's Kemp Town development. Every third house is articulated with giant Corinthian pilasters of a rusticated base. The composition centred on Russell's own house, Portland House; this was destroyed by fire in 1825 and rebuilt in a slightly different form. It no longer survives. The width of this house determined the width of the street in order that an uninterrupted view of the sea might be secured.

Montpelier Road was developed in stages from the 1820s. Numbers 53 to 56, shown here, are by Amon Henry Wilds; they are distinguished by the characteristic Ammonite capital on the pilasters, and shell heads to the first-floor windows. The Ammonite capital was first used in London by the architect George Dance; the name is derived from its resemblance to the volute of the fossil ammonite. Wilds doubtless used it as a pun on his own Christian name.

Montpelier Villas is a street of semi-detached houses in the picturesque Italianate style built from about 1845 to the designs of A.H. Wilds. Each house has a heavily rusticated ground floor with bow windows capped by bonnet canopies. The development is of great significance in Brighton as it was amongst the first to break away from the all-pervading terrace tradition. The Montpelier area was fashionable from the start. The author of *Brighton: The Road, The Place, The People* (1862), wrote: 'It so happened there resided at Brighton a certain family of the name of Jones, who feeling that there was not that tone of distinction attached to their surname . . .added thereunto their exact locality, and they called themselves, and were called by others, the Joneses of Montpelier'.

Montpelier Crescent was built between 1843 and *c*.1850 by A.H.Wilds on the site of a former cricket ground. The grandest of all Wilds' surviving works, the semi-detached villas are distinguished by a giant order of pilasters with either Corinthian or Ammonite capitals under a central pediment. The crescent was built in stages; numbers 7-31 came first, whilst numbers 1-6 and 34-38 were built in the 1850s. The Dials Congregational Church can be seen in the background of this picture taken in the 1950s.

Hanover Crescent was developed by an entrepreneur called Henry Brooker who, in 1814, employed A.H.Wilds to create a series of linked villas. The façades of some of the houses have been spoilt by the addition of attics. The group of three houses shown here have Wilds' characteristic Ammonite pilasters.

Clifton Terrace was completed in 1847 in a characteristic late Regency style. The terrace had the benefit of a private garden. The photograph, taken in the 1870s, shows the houses with bonnet-like canopies above angular bay windows. The front walls have attractive ironwork in the form of Greek anthemions. Today the railings have all gone, as have the valances on the canopies.

Park Crescent was developed on the site of a cricket pitch which formed part of James Ireland's Brighton Royal Pleasure Garden and Cricket Ground. The houses were designed by A.H.Wilds and built between 1849-54 in an Italianate style. On the garden side the villas are linked by three-storey towers with pedimented gables. Number 44 achieved notoriety when, in 1934, Toni Mancini murdered Violette Kay in the famous 'trunk murder'.

Powis Square in the 1950s. These bow-fronted houses were built in the 1850s; only the pediments above the central windows on the first floor, and the rather heavy balcony railings give any indication that these houses were not built 20 years earlier. The architect is unknown.

The drawing room, Grand Avenue Mansions, Brighton, photographed by the well-known architectural photographer Bedford Lemere in *c.*1890. The house was on land leased to the West Brighton Estate Company by Vere and Ellen Benett-Stanford of Preston Manor, Brighton. The company's architect was James Knowles.

Stanmer House, Stanmer Park, was built to the designs of Nicholas Dubois between 1721-27. The house was built for Henry Pelham, whose father, also Henry, bought the estate in 1713. The estate remained with the Pelham family, later Earls of Chichester, until 1947. The house is a Palladian composition with the central three bays emphasised by a pediment. The cornice and porch are later, and the single-bay extension on the right was added in 1860.

Patcham Place is one of the most impressive houses within the Borough of Brighton's boundaries. Situated west of London Road, it was originally built in 1558 for Sir William West; later in the century it was acquired by the Shelley family. The most notorious owner, however, was Anthony Stapley, who held the house from 1620. An adviser to Oliver Cromwell, he was one of the 59 MPs who signed Charles I's death warrant in 1648. In 1764 the house was refronted and remodelled for John Paine, in whose family it remained until 1926 when it was acquired by Brighton Corporation. It has been a youth hostel since 1939. The north front is entirely faced with black mathematical tiles.

This evocative photograph shows Moulsecoomb Place, the seat of the Tillstone family, in about 1890. Moulsecoomb Place was remodelled in about 1790 for Benjamin Tillstone. The early 18th-century house was faced in yellow brick, but the verandah looks *c.*1810. The house, together with its estate, was acquired by Brighton Corporation in 1925. For many years it was the headquarters of the Parks and Recreation Department. It is now owned by Brighton University.

Thomas Attree acquired the land which now forms Queen's Park in 1825. Inspired by Nash's Regent's Park and Decimus Burton's Calverley Park, Tunbridge Wells, Attree aimed to build a series of detached villas in their own grounds. The scheme was markedly different from contemporary Brighton developments such as Kemp Town and Brunswick Town, which were based on terraces. In the event only the German Spa, Cowell's Villa and Attree's Villa went up in Attree's lifetime. Attree's villa, shown here, survived until 1972; from 1909-66 it was occupied by a Xavierian Catholic boys' school. The villa was designed by Charles Barry in 1829-30 in an Italian Quattrocento style with a central loggia of arches supported on slender columns. All that survives today are some walls and gateposts in Queen's Park Terrace and Attree Drive, the villa's gazebo, seen to the left of the picture, and the famous 'pepperpot', built as a water tower.

The village of Rottingdean was annexed by Brighton in 1928. In the later 19th century it was frequented by artists and writers amongst whom was Sir Edward Burne-Jones. In 1880, Burne-Jones bought Prospect Cottage (far left in this photograph taken in about 1890); in 1889 he bought the adjoining property, known as Aubrey Cottage, and W.A.S.Benson built a new entrance with a studio above it. The two houses were renamed North End House, after Burne-Jones's London property. In 1923, Sir Roderick and Lady Jones (the latter better known by her pen-name of Enid Bagnold, the author of *National Velvet*) bought North End House and in 1927 they purchased the right-hand house, known as Gothic House. Since the death of Enid Bagnold in 1981, the right-hand part has been considerably altered.

The garden front of Preston Manor in 1909. The Manor was originally built in about 1250, rebuilt in 1738, and substantially added to and altered in 1905. On the deaths of Sir Charles and Lady Thomas-Stanford in 1932, the house and contents were left to Brighton Borough Council with the idea that the house should illustrate the way of life of an upper-class Edwardian family.

Vere Road was laid out following the passage of the Stanford Estate Act in 1871 which allowed Ellen Benett-Stanford of Preston Manor to grant building agreements on her 1,000 acre landholding in Brighton. In 1879, Charles Shelley bought sufficient land from the Stanfords to lay out nine houses. The Brighton architect and surveyor, Samuel Denman, provided the plans and elevations. Shelley's houses can be seen on the left of this Edwardian photograph. It is interesting to note that the houses have unpainted cement rendered façades which were intended to resemble Portland stone. The fashion for painting Victorian render dates from after 1945. The balustrades on the walls in front of the houses have all disappeared, and the gas lamp has been replaced by a 1930s swan-neck electric lamp. The road is named after Ellen Benett-Stanford's husband, Vere, who played a large part in the development of the Stanford Estate.

An unusual view of Brighton from the roof of St Bartholomew's Church in about 1940. To the left are the Southern Railway workshops, and in the distance can be seen the Preston Road viaduct, built in 1845-46. The serried ranks of terraced housing, developed from the 1870s, alarmed contemporary commentators. The *Building News* wrote in 1903: 'Visitors to the Southern watering-place, as they pass Preston, will find steep hills entirely covered with . . .brick and slate . . .they appear incrusted with a covering of stucco and slates, which is certainly not agreeable to the artistic sense. The rural charm of the green hillside has disappeared, and a dark coating of human habitations has taken its place.'

Widdicombe Way and Hodshrove Road, part of the East Moulsecoomb Estate, in 1938. This part of the estate was developed after December 1935 when 300 acres were acquired by the Corporation.

Waldegrave Road was built in a triangle of land between Preston Drive, Stanford Avenue, and Beaconsfield Villas. Like Vere Road (*qv*), the area was developed after 1871 on land owned by the Stanfords of Preston. The houses in this Edwardian postcard date from about 1890-1900; they typify the late Victorian terrace, with bays carried up to the first floor and gables projecting forward. Although the houses are narrow, they are quite deep and have back extensions. Note the uniform sash windows, unpainted cement render, wooden Venetian blinds, and front railings. The houses would have been largely rented before World War Two. Accessibility by train or bus, and the possession of Venetian blinds were features that were frequently stressed in contemporary advertising columns.

Nelson Street on 7 February 1935. One of a series of photographs taken in the 1930s by Brighton Corporation prior to 'slum' clearance work in the town. The Corporation commissioned a local photographer, Fawdry of 16a Dyke Road, 'principally to form a collection of records relating to clearance, and . . .to demonstrate those features of unfitness upon which the cases for clearance were based, *ie* most of the photographs demonstrated elements of disrepair, dampness, lighting, ventilation, sanitary arrangements, and bad arrangement . . .'

St John's Place, *c*.1930. A row of small early 19th-century cottages, one of which has a notice board announcing the availability of fresh cat and dog meat.

This fisherman's dwelling stood behind the present Marks and Spencer building in Western Road at 101 North Street. It abutted on to Haselgrove's forge and was approached through a narrow entry from Regent Row. The family had access to a common wash-house and water tap with several other households. The photograph dates from the 1930s.

Ivory Place on 7 February 1935, shortly before its demolition as part of the Morley Street redevelopment.

Photograph of Hayllar's Cottages looking west in January 1935. Access to this collection of ten cottages was from a narrow passageway on the southern side of Middle Street which passed under number 19 Middle Street. This property had been owned by Daniel Hayllar, hence the name.

Another atmospheric photograph of an area soon to be demolished. This view shows the rear of 8 Richmond Hill, looking towards Carlton Hill on 4 January 1935.

During the 1930s the Corporation undertook a major redevelopment of the area known as Albion Hill. The slopes stretching eastwards from Grand Parade had been developed during the first quarter of the 19th century and by the 1930s the closely packed houses in small back streets like Carlton Row, Nelson Row and Woburn Place, were regarded as seriously deprived areas. Demolition was commenced at the foot of Sussex Street (now renamed Morley Street). A new municipal market opened in Circus Street in 1937, a school clinic and infant welfare centre in 1938, and a chest clinic in 1936. Residents were rehoused in the four-storey Milner Flats built in 1934 and named after Alderman Hugh Milner Black. The Kingswood Flats, seen here a year after their completion in 1939, replaced Nelson Place and a primitive Methodist chapel in Sussex Street, which dated from 1856. The flats were named after the Minister for Health, Sir Kingsley Wood.

This view of King's Road is dominated by Embassy Court, designed by Wells Coates and D.Pleydell-Bouverie in the mid-1930s and built in 1934-35. Embassy Court was the first International Modern high-rise block in Brighton and was (and is) extremely controversial because of the way it intrudes into the Regency terraces along the seafront. When first built there were 69 flats on 12 floors; the tenth floor included the first penthouse flats to be built in England. The elevation has long bands of concrete between the windows which act as balconies. Where the glazing is flush with the concrete bands, sun rooms were provided with subtle curves to the windows. The flats were provided with all electric services, including space heating from ceiling panels, and unlimited hot water supplied by a thermo storage system in the basement.

Whitehawk Crescent, *c.*1930. This was initially developed by the Corporation in the late 1920s prior to the development of the large Council estate between 1933-37. Since 1975, Whitehawk has been largely rebuilt.

Newly erected houses in East Moulsecoomb in July 1937. The land for the estate was acquired by the Corporation in December 1935.

Recently erected flats on the Hollingbury Estate around 1950. They are typical of their type with steel-framed windows, known as crittalls. The Hollingbury Council Estate was developed following World War Two and building continued until 1964.

There was a housing shortage after the war and to counter the problem some properties built on the Hollingbury Estate were designed to be initially used as flats. These houses had a one-bedroomed ground-floor flat with a two-bedroomed flat above. When the housing situation eased, they could be converted into a three-bedroomed house.

The living room of 80 Moulsecoomb Way, *c*.1930. This appears to be an idealised view of what the interior decoration of a house should be, almost like a show-house. The young lad is smartly dressed and surrounded by furniture and fittings all of the same date.

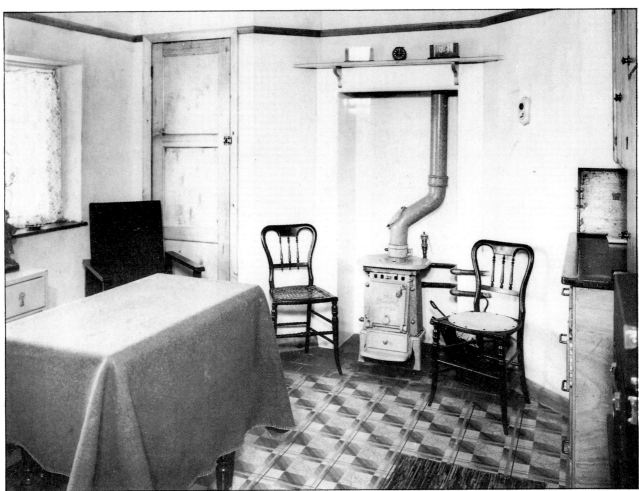

The sparsely furnished kitchen of a two-bedroomed flat on the Carden Avenue estate in June 1947. Note the mixture of old and new furniture.

The living room of a three-bedroomed house in the Carden Avenue estate in June 1947. The photograph may well illustrate a model house.

The combined kitchen and living room of one of the Carden Avenue flats in June 1947. Increasingly electricity was revolutionising women's role in the home. This kitchen has an electric iron on the shelf above the gas stove.

Shopping

Cowley's bun shop, Pool Valley, is one of Brighton's most famous surviving early buildings. It was built in 1794 and for 150 years was occupied by the Cowley family and used as a bakery. The three angular bays are faced with mathematical tiles, a characteristic Brighton feature. These were hung on timber-framed buildings to give the appearance of brick. Goodhart-Rendel commented that Cowley's was 'as charming a relic of the Brighton that was called Brighthelmstone as anyone could wish to see'. The shop has changed use since the photograph was taken in the 1950s.

Market Street in the early 1950s. The premises occupied by J.S.North and the Pump House Tavern are some of the oldest surviving buildings in the Lanes; the mathematical tiled fronts and bow windows are early 19th-century additions. Today, modern glazing bars have been inserted into the two bow windows and the canted bay on the right has been altered to form a bow window similar to the other two.

Needham's Ladies' Outfitters in about 1929. This impressive late Regency building with giant Ionic pilasters replaced the Castle Hotel, which was demolished in 1823. Originally built for residential use, it was later adapted for shops. It was demolished in 1930 and replaced by new shops and an electricity showroom. The site is now occupied by the Royal Bank of Scotland. During the heyday of Needham's, in the early 1920s, a fanfare of trumpets sounded from the roof at opening and closing time.

The north side of Duke Street opposite the junction with Middle Street. The photograph dates from before 1867 when the row of buildings on the right, which abutted on to the southern side of Holy Trinity Church, were removed as part of a road widening scheme. The clock tower was known as Schenk's clock after Frederick Schenk, a Geneva watchmaker who had occupied these premises for the previous 20 years. Further up the street demolition has already taken place and an area of fenced-off ground awaits sale and development.

The junction of Middle Street and Duke Street in 1868. When Duke Street was widened the previous year the trees were left in the centre of the road. Here they are in the process of being removed. On the left the façade of the Union Charity School, erected in 1807, is just visible. Prominent on the corner is a fine classical building occupied by Thomas Phillips, grocer and wine and spirit dealer. R.Reed at 7 Duke Street, is recognisable as a butcher's by the row of carcasses hanging outside.

Looking up West Street towards the Clock Tower around the turn of the century. The western side of the street is now completely different as virtually all the buildings were demolished between 1928 and 1938 to allow for road widening, the only exception being St Paul's Church which was set back from the road line and therefore was not affected. Ironically, the western side of West Street had already been redeveloped in the 1820s. On the other side of the street a few 18th-century houses remain today. West Street, as the name suggests, had originally marked the westernmost extent of the town of Brighthelmstone.

West Street looking north from the junction of King's Road in the early 1920s. At this date the street was still very narrow as demolition of the buildings on the eastern side did not commence until 1928.

The west side of West Street looking north in the mid 1920s. The buildings are clearly very run down and demolition was to sweep them all away before the 1930s were over. Note the off-street car parking on offer in Potts Garage — only 6d for two and a half hours.

West Street looking south towards the sea in 1931 prior to the commencement of further road-widening demolition work. The photograph shows how narrow West Street was. Between 1928-38 the western side of the street was demolished in stages.

London Road was developed in the 1820s as a residential district known, until 1826, as Queen's Road. The front gardens of the Regency villas had, by 1903, virtually all been converted into shops. Although the shops have all changed, the once elegant houses seen in this photograph taken in the late 1940s still survive.

Meeting House Lane in about 1948. The area of Brighton known as 'The Lanes' is a dense network of streets that formed part of the old town of Brighton until the mid-18th century. In design and layout these narrow alleyways have something of the atmosphere of the medieval town, though none of the houses predate the 17th century, and most date from the 18th, 19th and 20th centuries. In the later 18th century, the area was occupied by workers' houses which, a century later, had become run-down and shabby. In the 1930s, Sir Herbert Carden proposed a comprehensive redevelopment of the site; fortunately this was not carried out and the picturesque charm of The Lanes was increasingly appreciated. Today, the whole area has been rather self-consciously prettified and redeveloped.

In this photograph only the group of buildings on the immediate left survive in anything like a recognisable form.

Numbers 41-43 North Street in 1862. These were located on the south side of the street, just above Ship Street. The buildings are about to be demolished, hence the fly posters. The site was then occupied by W.J.Smith, who remained here until 1912. In the foreground is one of the town's gas lamps. Gas lighting in the public streets commenced in the Steine in 1824 and by the date of this photograph there were about one thousand gas lamps in the town. The first electric lights were experimented with in 1881, but gas lamps were still to be found in The Lanes in 1939.

The junction of Market Street and Brighton Place c.1890, a view that is recognisable today. The Sussex Hotel (now Tavern) fronts both East Street and Market Street and was known until 1816 as the Spread Eagle. Witherden's furnishing ironmongers occupied this site for some 20 years from the early 1870s.

A dramatic view of the crowded shop front display of Massey's ironmongery emporium at 10 Guildford Road as it appeared in January 1898. Amidst the items for sale are brooms, brush heads, wash-boards, stoneware hot water bottles, kettles, coal scuttles, water jugs and watering cans. The impressive lamp shows that Massey also retailed kerosene safety oil at 10d per gallon for use in oil lamps — the principal means of lighting a home.

Around the turn of the century Dunn's carpets and furnishing drapery store stood at the southern end of Trafalgar Street adjoining St George's Place. The firm first occupied this site in the late 1880s. The displays of rolled carpets, linoleum and rugs overflowed on to the pavement. The large first-floor display window was typical for shops of this date in tending to attract the eyes of passing trade travelling on the upper floor of the trams. Trafalgar Street developed in the 1840s following the construction of the railway station.

St George's Place consists of a short terrace of bow-fronted houses built in the 1820s and attributed to Wilds and Busby. Subsequently they have vitually all lost their verandahs and ironwork.

Black Lion Street looking north c.1900. In the foreground Holder Brothers china and glass showrooms are advertising their closure. The site was soon to be covered by the enlarged and rebuilt market building, designed in red brick and terracotta with glass and iron. Beyond Hodlers stands Burroughs Mineral Water Manufactory.

Lower's dining and tea room at 2-3 Market Street at the turn of the century. Here 'good accommodation' was to be had by visitors for 'moderate charges'.

Monsieur A.Boucher's Photograph Studio at 15 King's Road, *c.*1880. Boucher was a high-society photographer in Brighton between 1871 and 1885, first at studios in Ship Street, and then later in King's Road. His shop is decorated with a fine collection of photographic portraits. The lamps and canopy on the right are in front of Markwell's Hotel.

An 1890s view of the H.C. Treacher's bookshop, library and stationers on the corner of East and North Streets. The building was rebuilt in 1924 and is now occupied by part of Hannington's department store.

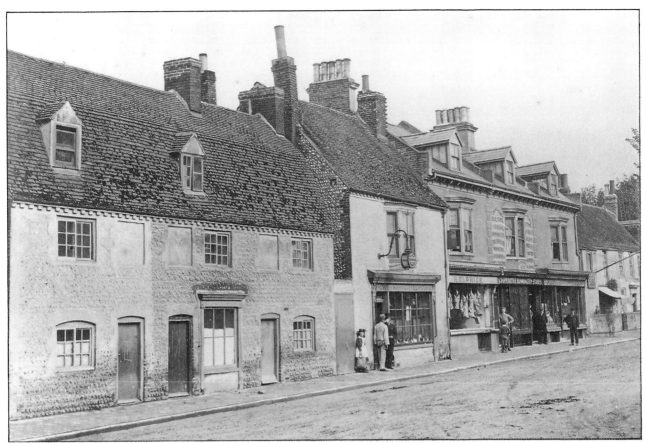

The parish of Preston was municipally linked to Brighton in 1873. This attractive group of houses and shops survived until 1894-95 when the area was redeveloped by the architect Charles Stanley Peach for Vere Benett-Stanford of Preston Manor. The view is of Preston Road, opposite Preston Manor.

The junction of Preston Road and South Road in about 1880. The walls of Preston Manor can be seen on the right.

East Street looking towards the Royal Pavilion, *c.*1895. A wide range of Brighton's people are represented here. In the foreground two working women, on the left a smartly-dressed middle-class lady passes a group of road menders. On the right a rather portly policeman seems intrigued by something out of the photograph.

East Street looking towards Pavilion Buildings and the south gate of the Royal Pavilion, *c.*1895. Pavilion Buildings were erected in 1852-53. In front of them a horse bus is waiting to depart.

St James' Street, *c*.1895. Initially developed in the 1790s and running parallel to the seafront, it is the main shopping street of the eastern part of the town. German Place on the right was renamed Madeira Place at the height of anti-German feeling during World War One.

Looking down North Street from the junction with Ship Street *c*.1910. The colonnade is visible on the left. The original colonnade had been erected outside the Theatre Royal in 1806-07 but it was extended around the corner as far as 157 North Street. It was largely removed in stages between 1912 and 1929, leaving only the small section in New Road. Beyond the colonnade the impressive façade of the Leeds Permanent Building Scoiety, designed by Clayton and Black in 1904 for the Royal Insurance Company, is prominent at the junction with New Road. Just beyond is the clock tower added to the Chapel Royal in 1882.

The colonnade in front of 157-159 North Street photographed in about 1925. A Doric colonnade was built in New Road in front of the Theatre Royal in 1806-07; this was carried round into North Street in 1823 though the architect, Thomas Cooper, changed the order from Doric to Ionic. In 1929 the colonnade was demolished for road widening.

Opposite page:
North Street in the 1920s.

Western Road, Brighton, in 1904 between Crown Street and Marlborough Street. The block was occupied by Carter Brothers, printers and bookbinders, an umbrella repairer, Bushell, and George Mense Smith, a general supplies dealer. The buildings were demolished and replaced by the Art Deco C & A building as part of the general widening of the north side of the road carried out between 1928-36.

William Hetherington's store on the corner of Preston Street and Western Road c.1905. Western Road was much narrower then with little room for traffic like the approaching open-topped horse bus to pass. It was also too narrow for trams to operate. This block of buildings, although altered, are still standing, those on the north side of the street were demolished for road widening in the years either side of 1930.

Western Road looking east in 1905. On the right are Castle Street and Clarence Square.

An Edwardian view of the southern side of Western Road looking towards the junction with North Street. Western Road developed in the first half of the 19th century as an important shopping street for the high-class residential areas that had grown up on either side. Increasingly shop fronts were built in the front gardens of the larger houses and by the 1860s the road had become the shopping street it is today. In the midst of this block of buildings, at number 40, was the birth place of the local inventor, Magnus Volk. The shops themselves exhibit the modern plate glass windows typical of the period and nearly all have exterior gas lighting to illuminate the windows at night.

Western Road was originally very narrow and a major widening scheme took place between 1928 and 1936. This shows the view in August 1934 and is taken from the junction with North Street and Dyke Road looking west. Clearly visible on the right is the glass roof of the Imperial Arcade. The buildings on the other side of the road vanished in 1967 with the development of Churchill Square.

The former Cork Shop in Gardner Street just prior to its closure in 1983. Established in 1883, the shop specialised in the manufacture of corks for a variety of purposes. The shop was re-assembled in Brighton Museum in 1984.

The North Road premises of the Brighton Equitable Co-operative Society in the early years of this century. The Society was founded at a meeting at a coffee shop in Duke Street on 26 November 1887. Under its first president, George Holyoake, a store was opened at 32 North Road in May 1888. Initially a small society, membership had not reached one thousand by 1900. In that year, 96 London Road was acquired as a main office and adjacent properties were purchased in 1909.

The premises of T.J.Braybon, gas fitter and plumber, at 106 East Street in 1897.

The staff pose in the doorway of Thomas Kilmister's boot and shoe shop at 137 North Street in the early years of this century.

The staff pose proudly outside Greenyer's ironmongers and general provision stores at 22 St George's Road, Kemp Town. The proprietor can be seen proudly posing with his 11 staff, set apart by his straw hat, stiff collar and jacket pulled back to reveal his watch chain. The impressive lamps advertise the wide range of goods held in stock.

The junction of Western Road and North Street in 1926. On the left is Soper's drapery store. The building dominated by the Bovril advertisement was soon to be demolished as part of the Western Road road-widening scheme.

This view of the west side of Queen's Road in May 1930 shows how much the introduction of local planning controls and the general limitations on the size and position of advertising hoardings has had on the streetscape of Brighton. Many of the products advertised are still familiar today but the cinema posters reveal that sound was still a relatively new experience for cinema audiences. The Palladium even had separate screen performances for silent films and for those with sound.

The interior of the Pavilion Creamery restaurant at 6 and 7 Pavilion Buildings in the early years of this century. Alf Duomo's restaurant now occupies the site.

Brighton Co-operative Society's main store in London Road was only four years old when this photograph was taken in 1935. Designed by Bethell and Sumnnel, the store has an 180ft frontage and was designed on four floors.

In the early 1930s there was much housing development in the valleys surrounding Brighton, particularly in Patcham, Whitehawk, Ovingdean and Falmer. To the east of the Falmer Road piecemeal development continued into the 1960s. This photograph was taken in October 1933 and shows Miss A.Chapman's small tobacconist and confectionery shop. Situated in Downs Road, Woodingdean, Miss Chapman offered a range of goods including 'Freshly made tea, coffee, cakes and Woodingdean Rock'.

Western Road, named after the Western Family of Preston Manor, became the town's principal shopping street from the 1820s. Between 1926-36, major street widening was carried out and new shops and department stores were built. Stafford's store, shown here in a photograph of about 1936, dates from about 1930. It is built in a characteristic '30s neo-classical style. Note the attractive flambeaux along the façade.

The south side of Western Road looking towards North Street in about 1930. The block of shops on the right was tragically demolished
in 1964-65 to make way for Churchill Square.

Business, Trade and Industry

A capstan and fishing boats on the beach, c.1890.

Brighton's fish market lay on the beach at the end of East Street. The fishing industry was in decline throughout the 19th and 20th centuries; by the turn of the century, however, there were still 88 fishing boats registered from Brighton, although this had fallen to fewer than 50 after World War Two. By the 1880s, the extension of the King's Road arches led to the creation of an area for the market stalls. This remained a popular attraction for visitors who enjoyed watching the catch being sold by Dutch auction. Mixed amongst the fishing barrows are tea and coffee vendors. Although in the latter stages fish was brought in from outside and sold wholesale, the market continued to operate until 1960 when it was removed to a new building in Circus Street.

Fishermen working on nets on the beach between Black Lion Street and Market Street in the late 1860s. The tarred huts were used to store fishing tackle and nets. Behind them the wooden fencing in the King's Road was replaced by iron railings in the 1880s.

Fishing boats jostle with bathing machines on the beach at the front of West Street in the 1880s. Nets are hung over the wooden rails of King's Road.

A rare glimpse of some of Brighton's fishermen standing in front of some of the King's Road arches used to store nets and equipment. The photograph dates from around the turn of the century.

Stallholders selling shellfish on the beach at the foot of West Street in May 1890. Behind stands the Shelter Hall, opened in August 1887. The large interior could hold 500 people and was used for events such as the luncheon following the inauguration of the Volk's 'Daddy-Long-Legs' railway in 1896.

Brighton fishermen equipped as divers, with the Chain Pier in the distance, c.1890.

Fred Collins's *Skylark* prepares for another pleasure trip towards the end of the 19th century. In the background are fishing boats.

Andrews' fishing tackle shop in Bartholomews in 1935. It was built in the late 18th century and was very typical of its kind.

Richmond Dairy Farm in the third quarter of the 19th century. Operated by the Chate family, this stood on the north side of Richmond Street on the site now occupied by Chates Farm Court.

A chestnut seller in the streets on 20 October 1934. He operated on the corner of Church Street and Regent Street.

A one-man-band performs in Brighton in September 1950.

The market buildings, photographed here in 1939, were designed by Francis May in 1900-01 in a Free Renaissance style which, as Pevsner has pointed out, seems to owe much to contemporary London Underground stations. The red brick and terracotta building was used for selling fruit and vegetables; the southern part (*qv*) was used as a floral hall. The market was demolished in 1940, though the façade remained until 1987.

The Floral Hall, Market Street, was built in 1901 by the Borough Surveyor, Francis May, as part of the reconstruction of the market building. The exterior was in a Free Renaissance style, whilst the interior boasted a waggon-shaped glass roof resting on arched girders. It was demolished in 1940.

The Sun Insurance Office, North Street, was demolished in 1930. This photograph, taken in 1929, shows an attractive group of buildings distinguished by a fluted Greek Doric colonnade at ground-floor level.

The east side of Queen's Road in the 1930s at the junction with North Road. The advertising hoardings mask the headquarters of the Moon Society for the Blind, where books and magazines for the blind were printed using a form of embossed print invented by Dr William Moon. Advertisement hoardings were a common feature of many streetscapes before the introduction of stricter planning regulations. If many of the products have not changed, the form of advertising has. Adjoining the Moon Society is the Cambridge Hotel and on the other side of North Road is the Brighton, Hove and Preston Dispensary designed by Herbert Williams in 1849 and closed in 1948.

Queen's Road was constructed in 1845 to improve access to the station. It soon became lined with shops, hotels, public houses, and warehouses. In 1875, the Brighton architect Samuel Denman built the large warehouse of the Pantechnicon Company whose twin towers crowned by cupolas are just visible in the photograph. The road was widened in 1878. This photograph was taken in 1931.

The interior of the National Telephone Company's central exchange at 39 Duke Street. Brighton had the first telephone exchange on the south coast, which opened in 1882 in West Street. This was operated by the United Telephone Company, whose local agent was the inventor Magnus Volk. In 1889 the major telephone companies amalgamated to form the National Telephone Company. By 1905 there were over 3,000 subscribers in the town. A short-lived rival municipal telephone system was established in 1903 but it was bought out by the Post Office in 1906, who also took over the National Telephone Company in 1912.

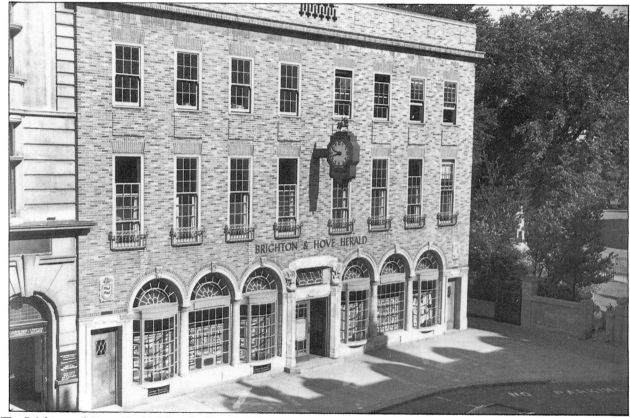

The *Brighton and Hove Herald* Office, Pavilion Buildings, was designed by John Leopold Denman and built in 1932-34 in a refined neo-Georgian style. The building is in brick with Portland stone dressings; the decorative carving was executed by Joseph Cribb of Ditchling. The offices now house the Royal Insurance building.

Prince's House, North Street, was built in 1935 by H.S.Goodhart-Rendel as the head office of the Brighton and Sussex Equitable Permanent Benefit Building Society. It is one of the finest 20th-century buildings in Brighton, constructed at a time when Goodhart-Rendel was influenced by the Modern Movement. Great subtlety is shown in the way the building turns the corner and in the decorative treatment of the cladding materials. The hand-made bricks are arranged in panels and punctuated with blue mosaic inserts. The building now houses the Norwich Union Insurance Group; the entrance has been considerably altered.

The Tower Mill close to Ditchling Road, *c.*1893. By this date the mill was in the ownership of C.Cutress and Son, whose Round Hill Road shop can be seen adjacent to the mill. When built by John Ingledew in 1838, the windmill cost £2,000; it was demolished in 1913 and Belton Road now marks the site.

Mitre House, Western Road, was designed by J.Stanley Beard and Bennett and built in 1935 by the International Stores which occupied part of the ground floor. The remainder of the building was (and is) devoted to flats and offices. The façade is functional, but the balconies and entrance have distinct Art Deco touches.

The Regent Iron Foundry on the corner of North Road and Foundry Street, *c*.1890. At its peak the foundry employed over 100 workers and was responsible for providing many of the iron railings around the town, as well as drain covers, parts of the piers and the Trafalgar Street and New England Road railway bridges. The foundry operated from the early years of the 19th century until 1912. The site is now occupied by the Royal Mail sorting office.

Preston Circus in the 1890s. The Hare and Hounds public house on the right was originally built in the 1820s, but was refronted in about 1870. It was rebuilt in 1905. The photograph is dominated by the tower of Longhurst's Amber Ale Brewery, built in 1881 for the Stanford Estate Trustees by H.J.Lanchester. It was demolished in 1901; a cinema and fire station was later built on the site. In the distance can be seen the Stanford Arms, which still survives.

The horse-drawn delivery carts of Tamplins brewery parade in August 1934; they were soon to be replaced by motorised vehicles. Tamplin's Phoenix Brewery in Albion Street was built in 1821 to replace Richard Tamplin's Southwick brewery destroyed by fire the previous year, hence the name given to the new site. Tamplins were taken over by Watney's in 1953.

The Stanford Arms public house at Preston Circus in the 1930s.

The Unicorn Inn stood in North Street on the western corner of Windsor Street and bore the date 1597. It opened as an inn in the mid-18th century. This view dates from around 1890 just before the inn was rebuilt in 1892. This in turn was demolished in 1919 to make way for the Regent Cinema. The site now forms part of Boot's The Chemist.

The Sassoon Mausoleum, Paston Place, was built in 1892 by an as yet unknown architect for Sir Albert Abdullah Sassoon. Sassoon lived at 1 Eastern Terrace, and the mausoleum for his family was built on adjoining land. He was buried there in 1896, and his son followed in 1912. However, Sir Philip Sassoon sold the building in 1933 and had the bodies removed. During the war the former mausoleum was used as an air-raid shelter, and in 1953 it became part of the Hanbury Arms pub. It still survives as the Bombay Bar, a strange transformation from its original purpose. The Indian style of the mausoleum has obvious stylistic analogies with the Royal Pavilion. However, it is probable that Sir Albert was referring less to Brighton's peculiar architecture than to the fact that the Sassoon family's trading empire was originally based in Bombay and later extended throughout the Near and Far East. The photograph was taken soon after the building ceased to function as a mausoleum.

Staff pose in front of the Tivoli Laundry delivery van. Laundry work was one of the main areas of employment for working women in the town during the 19th and early years of the 20th century.

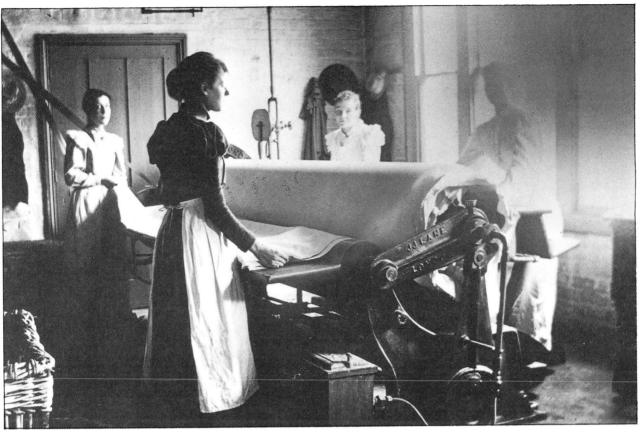

Removing the creases at the Tivoli Laundry in the late 19th century.

The interior of Reason and Company's Electrical Works in the Lewes Road, *c.*1912. The factory later became Allen West. They appear to be working on lamps for the seafront (*Information courtesy of Geoffrey Mead*).

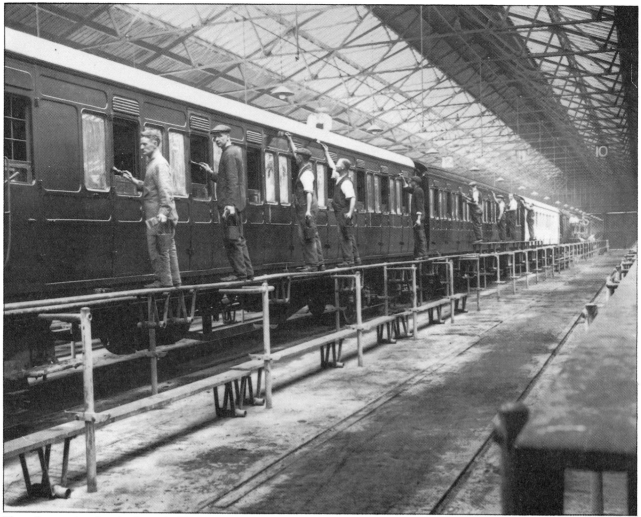

The railway paint shop in the early 1930s. This manually intensive work had ceased by the mid-1930s and the photograph may have been taken to commemorate this impending change. The paint shop, built in 1878 to the north of the Old Shoreham Road, was subsequently converted for use as an electric stock maintenance centre. The railway works were Brighton's major employer providing over 2,500 jobs at the end of the 19th century when the works stretched from the main line across the Old Shoreham Road. They were in decline from 1901 when the marine engineering section was removed to Newhaven. The works were partially shut in 1928 and the last locomotive was completed on 20 March 1957. A year later the works closed but the buildings were not demolished until 1969.

The Rival Lamps factory, opened on the Hollingbury Industrial Estate in 1950.

Demonstrators against high levels of unemployment in the town protest by blocking traffic outside the Brighton Labour Exchange in London Road on 4 January 1939. Unemployment was high in Brighton throughout the 1930s.

A fate that has befallen all too many of Brighton's buildings in the 20th century. On 15 October 1939, the crew of Lasensby Brothers, house breakers of 84 Trafalgar Street, proudly pose in front of their handiwork. Behind them are the partially demolished remains of 37 Market Street. Brighton has lost a number of architecturally significant buildings including the Central National Schools in Church Street, the Regent Cinema, and the Attree Villa in Queen's Park. The quality of the new buildings rarely matches those they replaced.

A road repair team at work in Western Road in the late 1890s.

Transport

View of Brighton Station from Queen's Road, *c.*1905. David Mocatta's original Italianate station front of 1841 still survives in a mutilated form behind the enormous *porte-cochère* erected in 1882-83.

Brighton Station in about 1906. This view shows the magnificent arched train shed designed by H.E.Wallis and erected in 1882-83. The shed is on a curve (like York) and is one of the largest of its kind. The station clock, which still survives, was added at the same time.

An Edwardian view of the locomotive sheds and marshalling yards. The engines are already coaled up. Brighton was the 'Swindon' of the London, Brighton, and South Coast Railway.

The *Southern Belle* celebrates its 21st anniversary on 1 November 1929. In return for a one-shilling supplement passengers could enjoy what was claimed to be 'the most luxurious train in the world'. A year after electrification in 1933, the train was renamed the *Brighton Belle*.

A busy Queen's Road looking north towards the junction with North Road during the 1890s. Queen's Road was constructed in 1845, using money from the railway company, to link the station with North and West Streets. As the main link between the station and the sea, it soon became lined with shops, hotels and public houses. The houses still have front gardens. Amidst the traffic is a horse bus heading down from the station and a milk cart heading in the opposite direction. The preponderance of horse-drawn traffic in the Victorian period led to problems, particularly during hot summers. At its peak in 1902, the horse population of Britain reached three and a half million; this produced an estimated ten million tons of horse droppings a year and caused a major public hygiene problem.

This wagonette called the *Brighton Belle* stands in the King's Road at the foot of West Street in 1895, waiting to depart to the Devil's Dyke. Wagonettes were a type of open carriage consisting of one or two seats arranged crossways at the front, the rest of the seats arranged lengthways and facing inwards. They were used for excursions. Until 1876 they were unlicensed and their proliferating numbers caused a considerable nuisance. In 1875, 30 wagonettes operated but the following year only 16 wagonette licenses were issued. By 1895 there were 60 operating within the borough.

Laying the tram rails in Marlborough Place in 1901. Brighton's trams were inaugurated along this stretch on 25 November 1901, but the system was not completed until 1904. The two-storey bow-fronted Georgian building in the centre of the picture housed the King and Queen public house. Probably dating from the late 18th century, when the first development of Marlborough Place, then known as North Row, commenced, the inn catered for the cricket ground on the North Steine, as well as the infantry barracks then located in Church Street. Brighton's corn market was held in the King and Queen until October 1868 when it transferred to the Corn Exchange. The existing building with timber framing, herring-bone brickwork and stained glass replaced this building in 1931-32.

The ceremonial opening of the tramway system on 25 November 1901 with the Mayor, Alderman John Stafford, driving car number one which had been suitably adorned for the occasion. The first route was from the terminus at the seaward end of Victoria Gardens along the Lewes Road to Preston Barracks. The tramway system operated by the Corporation was complete by July 1904 with a total of nine and a half miles of track.

An Elm Grove tram decorated for the peace day celebrations following the end of the Boer War. The initial Class A trams had open tops with reversed stairs, a wire mesh lifeguard on the front to prevent anyone falling under the vehicle, and an expanding lattice platform gate leading into the car. All were intended as safety features. The reversed staircase was to prevent passengers climbing to the top deck being thrown off the rear of the car as the driver accelerated.

London Road in about 1905. The shops to the right were largely demolished in the 1920s and 1930s. The tram was supplied in 1902 for the Corporation tramways. It was scrapped in 1926.

One of Brighton's first motor buses seen on the Steine in January 1904. The Milnes-Daimler 20hp bus was driven by Mr A.Dunn; the conductor was George Tongue. The first motor buses were introduced on the route between Hove Town Hall and Castle Square on Christmas Eve 1903. Fares on the open-topped, solid-tyred buses were relatively cheap, but the ride was not very smooth. By 1913 the Brighton, Hove and Preston United Omnibus Company was running six motorised routes but horse-drawn buses continued running until 1916. The bus is advertising Hannington's, the Brighton department store in North Street.

In 1912 both Brighton and Hove Corporations gained permission to operate trolley buses in response to moves by the United Omnibus Company. Trials were carried out in December 1913 but were brought to a halt by the outbreak of war. This view shows the Cedes-Stall Experiment in progress along Goldstone Villas in August 1914. There was great concern over the safety of 'trackless' cars and supporters hired the Dome in January 1912 to show film of them in action in Bradford and Leeds to allay public fears. Subsequently, Hove ratepayers voted 1,755 to 825 in favour of a trial. Contemporary newspaper reports record 'the greatest secrecy was observed as to the arrangements, but, of course, it was impossible to conceal the double-decker trolley bus when it appeared in the public streets, and as soon as the vehicle was observed careering down George Street, considerable crowds of people assembled . . .' They were regarded as noisy since they made a hissing noise when stopping and this, allied to the outbreak of war and the Austrian origins of the trolley-bus firm, put paid to their chances. The vehicle and system was bought by Keighley where they remained in use until May 1922.

Rows of private-hire buses in New Road off-loading children outside the Court Cinema in 1930. Just visible on the far right is the façade of the Central National Schools in Church Street.

In 1905, Harry Preston, the proprietor of the Royal York Hotel, was the chief instigator in getting tarmac laid on the Madeira Drive, from the Palace Pier to Kemp Town, so that it could serve as an occasional race-track. The usual road surface then in use was either crushed stone, wooden blocks or brick, none of which was very suitable for the increasing numbers of motor vehicles. Brighton's first motor week was held on Madeira Drive in July 1905 and proved a great success. Many famous motoring pioneers took part including C.S.Rolls, Clifford Earp and Theodore Schneider. Here the winner of the Autocar Challenge Cup, S.F.Edge, is seen in his 90hp Napier. Over a measured mile he exceeded 97 miles an hour. The *Brighton Gazette* described the sound of the cars' engines as like 'the sound of an artillery volley'.

Speed trials along Madeira Drive in 1935. Madeira Terrace and Marine Parade above provided a perfect grandstand to view the racing.

The invention of the motor car was to revolutionise life in Britain. The first motor car was imported into Britain in 1894. Two years later many of the restrictions imposed on road vehicles, including the need for a man to precede the vehicle carrying a red flag, were lifted and the speed limit was raised to 14mph. To celebrate, a procession of 30 cars started from London on 14 November 1896; 17 of them successfully completed the journey. Here the cars are seen on their arrival outside the Hotel Metropole.

The London-Brighton Veteran Car Run is now an established highlight of the year, but it only became a regular annual event towards the end of the 1920s. This photograph dates from 1927 and shows a 1903 Oldsmobile and a 1905 Cadillac. The Veteran Car Run was commemorated in the film *Genevieve* with Kenneth Moore, John Gregson, Dinah Sheridan and Kay Kendall.

These semaphore traffic signals were installed at the foot of West Street in December 1927 to cope with the rising tide of traffic. They were operated by a policeman occupying a raised platform in the centre of the junction. Further sets were installed at Preston Circus in 1928 and in Castle Square the following year. They were replaced by traffic lights in 1933. In the background is the Victoria Hotel, a building lavishly decorated with terracotta. Opened in 1882 as the Orleans residential club, it became the Victoria Hotel in 1898.

Initially the motor car was the preserve of the rich and it was only in the inter-war years that mass production techniques, and cheaper credit, brought the car within reach of the middle classes. The number of cars on British roads increased ten-fold between 1919 and 1939 and motor garages became a common sight. Bromley's Garage was built in 1926 in Rottingdean Road, Black Rock.

The latest models are in stock in Newman's motor showrooms in Pool Valley in 1939.

The Brighton United Services Men's Club children's outing in 1929.

A charabanc full of members of the staff of A. Gooding and Sons, a firm of sheet metal workers and electrical engineers based in Upper Russell Street. This photograph was taken in June 1923 as they were about to depart on the company outing to Pulborough and recorded the firm's first ever annual outing by motor vehicle. All previous 'beanfeasts' had been by horse-drawn wagonette but on this occasion a charabanc of Southdown Motor Services was hired for the day.

Digging up the tram lines in the Lewes Road at the beginning of the war. Behind is one of the new fleet of trolley buses which operated on this route for 20 years from April 1939 until March 1959.

Recreation

Brighton race stand *c.*1861. Surprisingly this is not a race meeting but one of the mid-19th-century Easter Volunteer Reviews. They commenced in 1861 with 12,000 volunteer soldiers arriving by train and exercising on White Hawk Down. The highlight was a sham 'Battle of Ovingdean' on Easter Monday. The first Brighton Races were held in July 1783 and with royal patronage the races became a very fashionable event. The first wooden stand was built in 1788, burnt down in 1803 and replaced in the same year. By the end of the 1840s the races had lost their exclusivity as the railway brought less-desirable elements to the town for race week. A new organisation, the Race Stand Trustees, was established in 1849-50. In an attempt to revitalise the races, Allen Stickney, the Town Surveyor, designed this stand for them in August 1851. As attendances boomed, a southern wing was added in 1866, and a northern one in 1871.

In the 1930s, Brighton Corporation spent some £60,000 on improvements to the race course, and between 1930-38 a wide variety of new buildings were provided including this club stand, built in an Art Deco style in 1936 by Yates, Cook and Derbyshire of London. It no longer survives. The race course featured prominently in Graham Green's *Brighton Rock* (1938), where the infamous razor gangs are well described. The photograph was taken in 1946.

The Brighton YMCA Wrestling Club, 1907-08.

Six-a-side roller-skate football played between two teams of women in an unidentified Brighton skating rink in January 1907. The goals were six feet high and seven feet wide and to prevent the ball lifting it was filled with one pint of water. Roller-skating itself was in the midst of a revival in the Edwardian period. First invented with the appearance of ball-bearings in the 1870s, the initial wave of 'rinkomania' was short-lived. It illustrates the changing attitude of women in the years before World War One, as they increasingly participated in active sports like tennis and cycling.

The Bishop of Lewes (in top hat) watches Brighton and Hove Albion play Swindon Town on 23 April 1910. That year the 'Albion' won the Southern League championship and went on to defeat the Football League champions Aston Villa 1-0 at Stamford Bridge to win the FA Charity Shield. The forerunner to the Seagulls was called Brighton United; it was formed in 1898 and played in the Southern League. A professional team, they closed in 1900 and a number of new players went on to play for an amateur team, Brighton and Hove Rangers. They were accepted into the Southern League's Second Division, turned professional and became Brighton and Hove Albion.

Whitehawk won the Sussex Senior Cup in 1951. This photograph, however, shows action from the semi-final. Whitehawk Football Club were formed in 1945 and initially played in the Brighton League. Following their success in 1951 they joined the Sussex County League.

Members of the Brighton Swimming Club photographed outside the seafront arch they occupied from 1872. The photograph was taken at 8.00am on a March morning in 1881. Originally founded following a meeting held at The Jolly Fisherman in Market Street on 4 May 1860, the club claimed to be the oldest in the kingdom. The entry fee to the club was one shilling, with a weekly subscription of 2d, which may explain why there were only 13 members in the first year. These intrepid pioneers provided their first 'aquatic entertainment' in July 1861 with 'activities commencing at 6am'! Initially the club's headquarters was a shed on the Aquarium beach, but this was soon enlarged by using two disused railway carriages. With the commencement of the construction of the Aquarium in 1870, they lost their site and the club folded. Two years later it was revived, albeit under a different name, as the Brighton Aquarium Swimming Club, but the old name was soon reinstated. In this proud group the bewhiskered gentleman, fourth from the left in the second row, is George Brown one of the founder members of the club.

The North Road Swimming Baths under construction in 1895. The baths were open to men and women on separate days. They were closed in November 1979 and the new Regent Swimming Pool was built on the site. The entrance archway from North Road proclaiming 'Public Baths' still stands in North Road.

Black Rock swimming pool was designed by David Edwards, the Borough Engineer and built in 1934-36 in an unobtrusive Seaside Modern style. The pool was closed in 1979. The photograph shows the pool in its heyday in about 1938.

A dramatic night-time view of the entrance to Black Rock Swimming Pool, c.1936.

Black Rock bathing pool after World War Two.

The SS Brighton stood in West Street on the corner of Russell Road. Opened on 29 June 1934 as a swimming pool, the exterior was faced with cream tiles, whilst the interior was decked out like an ocean liner. The pool claimed to be the largest covered sea-water pool in the world and measured 165ft by 60ft. However, less than 15 months after opening, the pool was covered and converted to an ice rink, re-opening as the Brighton Sports Stadium. The first ice show was a ballet entitled *Viennese Memories*, based on the music of Strauss, which was first performed on New Year's Eve 1936. The stadium went on to host wrestling, judo, basketball and professional tennis, as well as becoming home to the Brighton Tigers ice hockey team. In September 1959 a change of ownership led to a change of name to the Brighton Palladium and to a change of use as a concert venue. This was short-lived and in 1962 the stadium reverted to its former use. Adjacent to the SS Brighton the new owners, Top Rank, had erected the Kingswest complex and so the stadium was closed in October 1965 and subsequently demolished. In 1990 the site was redeveloped and now houses a modern hotel.

A group of cyclists in the Old Steine, *c.*1877. The bicycle was introduced into Britain in the late 1860s and cycle clubs sprung up all over the country. Cycling provided moderate physical exertion but, because of the cost of equipment, remained slightly exclusive. By 1878, Brighton Cycling Club had 20 members. With the invention of the pneumatic tyre, cycling developed into a craze in the 1890s. Note particularly the female cyclist; at this date she was an intrepid pioneer but cycling came to be a symbol of emancipation for women towards the end of the century.

The entrance to Preston Park in about 1905. The gate piers and cast-iron gates were designed by Philip Lockwood, the Borough Surveyor, in 1883-84; the ironwork was cast by James Longley of Crawley. The impressive Park Superintendent's lodge lies to the left. Both gates and lodge were demolished in 1928.

Preston Park was formerly the private pleasure grounds attached to Preston Manor. In 1883, Vere and Ellen Benett-Stanford sold the land for £50,000 and the park was officially opened to the public in 1884. After its acquisition by Brighton Corporation, the park was landscaped by James Shrives together with the Borough Surveyor, Philip Lockwood, at a cost of £23,000. A councillor complained, however, that 'Mr Lockwood knew no more about landscape gardening than a cow did about a musket'. Winding paths meandered amongst scattered clumps of trees and carriage drives were laid parallel to London Road and Preston Park Avenue. In 1883, a policy of acquiring trees from famous people was initiated: both Gladstone and Lord Salisbury presented chestnuts from their estates. Plants were supplied from the Corporation Nursery, established at the Lewes Road waterworks in 1875. By 1904, no fewer than 117,000 bedded-out plants were being supplied in the summer to the town's parks and gardens. A similar number of spring flowers were also supplied. Preston Park, like other Victorian parks, had a specific moralising purpose. The *Brighton Gazette* commented: 'Parks are the best competition for public houses, and the grant of facilities for drinking in the pure air of heaven is the best way of supplanting the use of grosser stimulants'.

Public parks were seen as vital weapons in the war against drunkenness and disease, and as a means of civilising the working classes.

Design for a clock tower for Preston Park, 1891. The foundation stone of the clock tower was laid in August 1891 and the structure was completed in 1892. The tower, in red brick and terracotta, was designed by Francis May, the Borough Surveyor, in the fashionable 'Free Renaissance' style common for municipal buildings at the turn of the century. The base is inscribed: 'Here I stand, with all my might/To tell the hours by day and night/Therefore example take by me/And serve thy God as I serve thee.' The tower still survives in Preston Park.

The official opening of the rockery, Preston Park, by the Mayor, Councillor E.Denne, in May 1936. The rockery, built on the side of a railway embankment, was the largest municipal rock garden in Britain. It was designed by Captain B.Maclaren, the Park Superintendent, and work began in 1934; the inspiration reputedly came from a Chinese willow pattern plate. As much as 1,350 tons of stone was imported from Cheddar and unloaded from goods waggons at the top of the embankment. The three and three-quarter acre site was planted with 5,000 trees and 30,000 plants, of which 25,000 were alpines and 1,000 were water plants for the 100ft waterfall. In addition, a picturesque thatched tea room was built of stone from the police station on The Level, originally constructed in 1866. The total cost was £4,287. A celebrated municipal row developed when a local nurseryman, Arthur Pratt, suggested that Maclaren had paid too much for the stone. Only after a lengthy legal battle was Maclaren able to clear his name.

In 1928, Captain B.Maclaren initiated a campaign to remove all the 19th-century railings from Preston Park. This formed part of Sir Herbert Carden's plans to 'open up' the town's parks and open spaces; it can also be seen as a typically 1920s and 1930s reaction to all things Victorian. The picture, taken for the *Brighton Herald* in 1936, shows the removal of railings from Preston Park Avenue.

A view of the entrance to the Dome concert hall in 1910. The Dome was built by William Porden as the stable block to the Royal Pavilion between 1803-06. In 1867, it was remodelled by Philip Lockwood for use as a concert hall. Francis May provided a new *porte cochère* in 1901-02. To the right can be seen part of Brighton Museum, built by Lockwood in 1872-74. The bedded-out flowers were planted to commemorate the Coronation of George V.

The children's playground on the Level was laid out in 1927 and included, as this photograph shows, a boating pool, bridges and pergola.

The King and Queen Public House, Marlborough Place, was built on the site of a farmhouse which, in 1779, was granted a license to cater for sporting events on the North Steine. The inn was a simple two-storey bow-fronted building until 1931-32 when it was lavishly rebuilt in the Tudor style by the Brighton architects Clayton and Black. The interiors were fitted out by Ashley Tabb of Heaton, Tabb & Company, a well-known firm of pub decorators. The *Sussex County Magazine* commented in 1934: 'It is something more than a handsome, spacious building, wherein people can eat, drink, and be merry in perfect comfort. It is a gorgeous flight of architectural imagination.' Appropriately enough, the figures of George III and Queen Charlotte which decorated the façade of the old pub were replaced by carvings of Henry VIII and Anne Boleyn. The photograph was taken in 1934 for the *Brighton Herald*.

Barnum and Bailley's circus' visit to the town was preceded by a parade through the town on 13 July 1899. Here the parade of animals, performers and decorated floats is seen passing along Western Road, near Borough Street.

One of the cars of the Devil's Dyke suspension railway. This straddled the valley providing a hair-raising journey for up to eight passengers at some 1,200ft. It opened on 13 October 1894 and was operated by the Telpher Cable and Cliff Railway Syndicate Ltd. The journey took two minutes and cost 6d.

Theatres and Cinemas

The sad remains of the Oxford Music Hall following a destructive fire on 21 March 1867. This was one of several music halls in the town which provided cheap evening entertainment. Situated in New Road near the Theatre Royal, the Oxford was originally built in 1854 as Wright's Music Hall. Following the fire it was rebuilt as the New Oxford Music Hall which also burnt to the ground in 1892. Rebuilt again, it went through several name changes before being converted to a cinema in 1909. After the last war it became the Dolphin (then her Majesty's) Theatre before briefly flirting with film again between 1955 and 1957. It closed in 1963 and was demolished four years later.

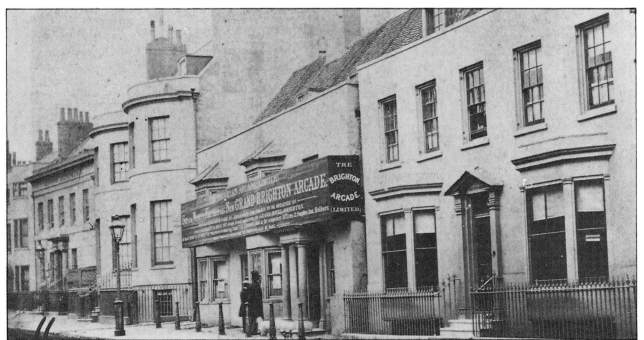

Number 78 West Street in 1865. The hoarding marks the impending demolition of this 18th-century house which had formerly been the home of Henry Thrale and played host to many famous literary guests including Dr Samuel Johnson and Fanny Burney. It was demolished to make way for the West Street Concert Hall, designed by Horatio Goulty.

The Paris Cinema, New Road, was built in 1892 in an elaborate French Second Empire style. It started life as the Empire Theatre, changed names several times, and in 1909 was converted into a cinema. It then alternated between a theatre and cinema, until in 1955 it became the Paris Continental Cinema. It closed in 1963 and was demolished in 1967 when it was replaced by an anonymous office block.

West Street looking north, *c.*1890. The tall building on the right was the Grand Roller-Skating Rink, opened in 1877 when the West Street Concert Hall was converted. The building later survived a couple of fires and a period of use as a cinema, until becoming Sherry's Dance Hall in 1919. After the war it reverted to being a skating rink and the façade was rebuilt in 1969. It is now an amusement arcade and nightclub.

An Edwardian view of the Hippodrome in Middle Street. The building first opened in 1897 as an ice-skating rink but in 1901 it was converted into a circus and theatre by the architect, Frank Matcham. Two hours of music hall could be enjoyed for 6d and many stars performed throughout its life including Sarah Bernhardt, Marie Lloyd, George Robey and Houdini. In 1964 the Beatles and the Rolling Stones attracted large audiences but it shut the following year and since 1967 it has been in use as a bingo hall.

The Palladium Cinema stood on King's Road at the junction with the former Russell Street. Built to the designs of Frank Matcham, it opened on 29 October 1888 as the Alhambra Opera House and Music Hall. The ornate interior seated 1,200 people. Later adapted for film, it reopened as the Grand Cinema de Luxe or Palladium Cinema on 6 April 1912. In 1936 a new Art Deco façade was built and the cinema changed its name to the Odeon, but only until the following year when the West Street Odeon opened. The Palladium finally closed in May 1956 and the site is now part of the Brighton Centre.

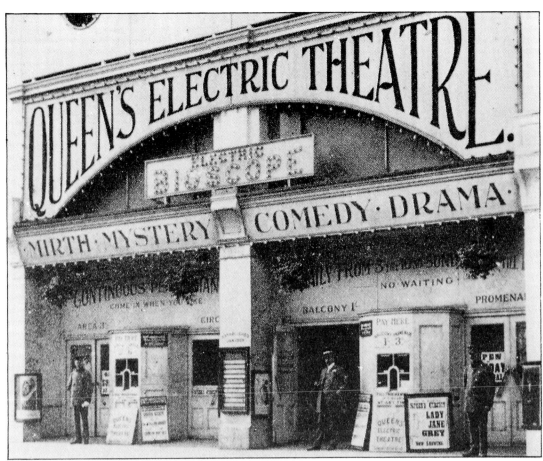

The Electric Bioscope opened on 13 January 1909 when an existing shop was converted into a small 50-seater cinema. Expanding into an adjacent property the following year, the name was changed to the Queen's Electric Theatre. With 250 seats, a pit orchestra, dimmed lights and drawn curtains, this has been called the town's first cinema.

The Academy Cinema decorated for the Jubilee of King George V and Queen Mary in 1935. Originally opened on 6 June 1911, the original cinema was rebuilt in 1913. The Academy finally closed on 24 January 1973 and the site is now marked by an office block, Academy House.

The Scala in Western Road soon after talking pictures were shown in March 1930. It opened in 1909 as the Electric Bioscope. Various name changes followed, including the Queen's Picture Theatre (1915), the Picturedrome (1919), the Scala (1922), the Regal (1932) and, after an Art Deco remodelling, the Curzon in 1936. Amongst the attractions were armless 'lovers' seats' in the circle. In 1975, a final name change to the Classic occurred before the cinema closed on 31 August 1979. The site is now marked by Waitrose's supermarket in Western Road.

The Rex News Theatre in North Road, Brighton, in 1938. Opened in 1911 as the Coronation Cinema, it became the New Coronation in 1928, the Roxy in 1934, and the Rex News Theatre in 1938. A small cinema seating 350 people in 1932, it became the last Brighton cinema to install sound. It closed in June 1939 but the building still stands at the eastern end of the road.

The Prince's Cinema, North Street, in 1933 following the introduction of a new foyer and neon-lit façade.

The Prince's News Theatre, North Street, on 4 February 1966. A cinema had first opened on this site in 1911 known as the Bijou Electric Empire. A series of name changes followed — the Prince's Electric (1915), the Bijou Select Palace (1918) and the Prince's Cinema (1919). It became the Prince's News Theatre in 1947, the Jacey in 1967 and the Brighton Film Theatre from 1969 to 1978. Its final incarnation was as the Cinescene until its closure in 1983. It has subsequently been refurbished as a fast food restaurant although evidence of its cinematic origins remain inside.

The Regent Cinema, formerly on the corner of North Street and Queen's Road, was designed by Robert Atkinson for the Provincial Cinematograph Theatre Ltd in 1921. The façade was decorated with tile panels designed by C.J.L. Doman and executed by George Jackson and Sons. Atkinson's design provided seating for some 3,000 people, and the cinema was widely considered to be one of the most luxurious in the country. In 1923, the Regent dance hall was opened on the site of the original roof garden. Six years later, after a fire had destroyed part of the auditorium, the cinema was reopened as Brighton's first 'talkie'. The photograph shows an aeroplane lent by the local aviation enthusiast, Graham Head, to advertise the film *Hell's Angels*. The cinema was closed in 1973 and tragically demolished in 1974. The site is now occupied by Boot's The Chemists.

Numbers 10-17 Gloucester Place in 1932-33, just prior to the commencement of demolition to allow for the erection of the Astoria Cinema. These houses were built in the opening decades of the 19th century and lost their front gardens only at the beginning of this century. On the far right is the Baptist Church built by George Barnes in 1904 to replace the Queen's Square Baptist Church. Note the attractive street lamp.

A photograph of the Astoria Cinema taken to publicise the personal appearance of Gordon Fellowes and Miss Marsh, *c.*1935. The Astoria Cinema in Gloucester Place was built to the designs of E.A.Stone; it could seat 1,823 people and included a restaurant, tea rooms and organ. It was opened on 21 December 1933 by Sir Cooper Rawson, MP, when the first film was *The Private Life of Henry VIII*. In May 1977 it ceased to be a cinema and became the Coral Social Club.

The interior of the lavish Regent dance hall in 1939. When the Regent Cinema first opened it had been intended to build a roof garden in the superstructure of the roof, but in November 1923 a dance hall was provided instead. The ballroom was lavishly decorated in keeping with the rest of the super-cinema. The dance hall became a bingo hall in 1967 and was demolished along with the rest of the cinema in 1974.

North Street looking north from Portland Street in the late 1930s. The block of buildings is ear-marked for demolition to allow for street widening.

The same view following the erection of the Essoldo Cinema and a shop-office complex on the land between Windsor Street and Portland Street. In April 1940 the Essoldo originally opened as the Imperial Theatre showing plays and variety shows. By 1943 it had become a cinema and films alternated with stage shows. From 1950 it was called the Essoldo and in 1964 it became a bingo hall. Beyond the Essoldo is the side entrance to the Regent Cinema.

The Kemp Town Odeon at the junction of Paston Place and St George's Road after World War Two. This cinema was built on the site of the Sassoon family's riding school and opened on 1 February 1934. With 900 seats it proved a popular venue. Tragically, on 14 September 1940 it was badly damaged in a mid-afternoon air-raid with four children and two adults killed, and 20 others injured. The Odeon closed in November 1960, was converted to a bingo hall two years later and, after a brief period in the 1980s as a social centre for the needy, it was demolished in January 1986 and a block of flats erected on the site.

The Imperial Theatre, North Street, on its opening night, 9 April 1940.

Wartime

During World War One the Royal Pavilion Estate was used as a military hospital, initially for soldiers from the Indian sub-continent, and later for limbless men. The first troops were admitted on 1 December 1914. By its closure in 1916 the hospital had seen 4,306 patients through its doors. Only 32 died in Brighton as the more gravely ill succumbed during the arduous journey from the Western Front.

Brighton General Hospital, Elm Grove, was originally the workhouse, built to the designs of George Maynard in 1865-67. Accommodation was initially provided for 861 inmates. In 1914 the workhouse changed its name to the Brighton Poor Law Institution, but on the outbreak of war the building became a military hospital which, between 1915-16, housed wounded Indian soldiers and, later, British troops. During this period it was known as the Kitchener Indian Hospital.

During World War One, women undertook many traditionally male jobs. Here a road repair team is seen posing in front of the Corporation traction engine in Ditchling Road. Significantly, the driver, William Harrop-Roller, and foreman, were still male.

The Prince of Wales (later King Edward VIII and then the Duke of Windsor) unveils the Indian war memorial, known as the Chattri, at Patcham on 1 February 1921. The Chattri was designed in white Sicilian marble by E.C.Henriques under the supervision of Sir Samuel Jacob. It was erected by the India Office and Brighton Corporation on the site of the 'ghat' (or place of cremation) for the Hindus and Sikhs who died in the Indian military hospital at the Royal Pavilion during World War One.

This rather sinister picture appeared in the *Brighton Herald* in August 1938 under the heading 'Brighton and Hove Welcome German Police'. In that year the Anglo-German Friendship League invited a party of 40 policemen from Wuppertal to visit Brighton and Hove. A football match was organised against a Sussex team and the game, according to the *Herald* was 'packed with lively and exciting incidents'. The Sussex team won by five goals.

British or Civic Restaurants were established in 1942 largely because the government was concerned about the quality of food available to the less well off. The restaurants were self-service and the food was cheap, with fixed-price menus at 10d or 1s (4p and 5p in today's currency). They were non profit-making and the government guaranteed them against loss. By 1943, some 2,160 had opened. The Civic Restaurant illustrated here was in the London Road and survived until 1945.

Interior of the Civic Restaurant, London Road, *c.*1943.

At the outbreak of World War Two, Brighton was earmarked as an evacuation area for children from London in the expectation of air-raids on the capital. September 1939 saw over 21,500 evacuees arrive in the town. However, with the increasing fears of German invasion following the collapse of France, Brighton was no longer regarded as safe and children were evacuated from Brighton. This column of evacuees are arriving in Brighton in 1939.

A class of school children practice wearing their gas masks. The fear of a gas attack was very real in the early part of the war. The intention was to get the children used to using their gas masks. The gas masks were carried in cardboard boxes which can be seen on the desks.

A bus waits at the traffic lights in the Old Steine in February 1943. In an attempt to save fuel this bus is operating with a trailing gas producer. Trolley bus operation had commenced just prior to the outbreak of war on 1 May 1939. They continued to operate after the war and the final run was made on 30 June 1961 on the Patcham to Fiveways route.

Two tanks caused quite a stir inside the Pavilion south gate in 1941.

An aerial view of Preston Park taken on 12 March 1948. Half of the park was dug up during the war for use as allotments to aid the war effort.

On 15 August 1945, soldiers and civilians alike celebrated VJ (Victory in Japan) Day outside the Sussex Hotel in East Street. The euphoria at the end of the war is clear. There was dancing in the streets and on the Pavilion lawns, and bonfires were lit on the beach as deck-chairs and beach huts were broken up for fuel.

A street party to celebrate the end of the war.

Rationing remained a feature of life after World War Two. Here a bread queue forms.

After the war, many items remained unavailable and luxuries were rationed. These children are clearly enjoying their ice-creams in Duke Street in July 1946.

A rather bizarre road safety campaign display on the back of a Corporation lorry.